MW00817842

Out in Front

Out in Front
Preparing the Way for JFK and LBJ

———————————— JEB BYRNE ————————————

excelsior editions
State University of New York Press
Albany, New York

Cover photo: President John F. Kennedy, Vice President Lyndon B. Johnson and others in the Texas trips' entourage walk to the podium for JFK's outdoor speech in Fort Worth in the early morning of November 22, 1963. The Fort Worth Press.

Published by
State University of New York Press, Albany

© 2010 State University of New York

All rights reserved

Printed in the United States of America

No part of this book may be used or reproduced in any manner whatsoever without written permission. No part of this book may be stored in a retrieval system or transmitted in any form or by any means including electronic, electrostatic, magnetic tape, mechanical, photocopying, recording, or otherwise without the prior permission in writing of the publisher.

For information, contact State University of New York Press, Albany, NY
www.sunypress.edu

Excelsior Editions is an imprint of State University of New York Press

Production by Diane Ganeles
Marketing by Fran Keneston

Library of Congress Cataloging-in-Publication Data

Byrne, Jeb.
  Out in front : preparing the way for JFK and LBJ / Jeb Byrne.
    p. cm.
  Includes index.
  ISBN 978-1-4384-3145-1 (hardcover : alk. paper)
  ISBN 978-1-4384-3144-4 (pbk. : alk. paper)
  1. Byrne, Jeb. 2. Political consultants—United States—Biography.
3. Kennedy, John F. (John Fitzgerald), 1917–1963—Friends and associates.
4. Johnson, Lyndon B. (Lyndon Baines), 1908–1973—Friends and associates. 5. United States—Politics and government—1961–1963.
6. United States—Politics and government—1963–1969. I. Title.

  E840.8.B967A3 2010
  324.70973—dc22
  [B]   2009030540

10 9 8 7 6 5 4 3 2 1

*This book is dedicated to the other
anonymous men of 1964*

Shun the Columns

Early in the election campaign, President Johnson called in his advance men and told them a story.

He recalled how he, as a young Congressman, worked for the reelection of President Franklin D. Roosevelt in 1940. Roosevelt had asked him to channel party funds and party workers to the crucial congressional districts.

Johnson told his advance men that Drew Pearson had written a column after the election, giving him credit for defeating Republicans in the House and swelling Roosevelt's vote.

Johnson said he was called to the White House the day the column appeared. Puffed up over the publicity, he expected to get Roosevelt's congratulations. Instead, Johnson quoted Roosevelt as saying:

"I see Drew Pearson has been praising you. I don't like to read the names of my confidants in the papers. Do you get the message?"

President Johnson paused after telling the story. Then he told his advance men: "Do you get the message?"

They got it and remained the most anonymous men in the Johnson campaign. . . .

From Drew Pearson's newspaper column,
November 8, 1964

Contents

Prologue

This is the story of the last hours of President John Fitzgerald Kennedy and of the course of action taken by his successor, Lyndon Baines Johnson, following President Kennedy's assassination. It is told from an unusual point of view, that of an advance man who served both Democratic presidents in the early 1960s in their quests for the nation's principal office: JFK to win election to a second term; LBJ to fill out JFK's unexpired term and seek election to a full term on his own.

This account could also be characterized as a political participant's memoir, focusing as it does on the actual practice of "advancing" during a pre-campaign and campaign for the presidency. The candidates and advance men dwelt on here were all Democrats. The period includes the shock wave of President Kennedy's death, indeed, it is shaped by that momentous and tragic event.

The vantage positions of the writer were advance man for JFK's pre-campaign appearance in Fort Worth, Texas, on the morning of November 22, 1963, advance man for LBJ on several pre-campaign travels in 1964, and deputy head of LBJ's advance unit in the 1964 campaign. There are also accounts of two post-election advances for the additional light they shed on presidential advancing generally.

The designation of "advance man" in the modern political context is the name given the campaign worker who precedes the candidate and makes an assortment of arrangements for the candidate's appearances on the campaign trail. He is literally out in front. His function is to prepare the way for the candidate, accentuate the positive, smooth the perceived rough spots, monitor the actual event, and make the candidate and his or her message look good—all aimed at winning an election. With a sitting president as a candidate that means the advance man must coordinate with the entire "apparatus" of specialists that a traveling president takes with him.

Variations of this vanguard function have been common in the past. One of my favorites, come upon while lightly rummaging through British history, was the "Knight Harbinger," forerunner for a royal progress, or what we would call a trip. Among his duties, we learn from George Herbert's poem *The Forerunners*, published in 1633, was chalking the walls of lodgings requisitioned along the route to guide courtiers in the royal train to their assigned chambers. I am sure he did much more. This knighthood, which could be considered a predecessor of the modern political advance man, lasted from the mid-1600s until 1846. I think latter-day political advance men would prefer to trace the activity in which they are engaged to the Knight Harbinger than to, say, the carnival advance man breezing into town with a roll of COME SEE THE DAREDEVIL ACT! posters under his arm and a pocketful of free passes for the ladies and gentlemen of the press. But that is an advance man for a somewhat different cause.

In American politics there have been conflicting traditions over whether presidential candidates should or should not campaign for themselves. William McKinley famously ran for president by sitting on his front porch and waiting for supporters to visit. This obviated the need for advance men as such. McKinley had the fabulous fundraiser and publicist Mark Hanna working for him, and that proved sufficient. The porch sitter easily defeated his frenetically traveling opponent, William Jennings Bryan.

In the present era, though, despite the multiple means of reaching potential voters, candidates for the presidency find it imperative to be constantly on the road to attract funds and votes. Personal appearances in favorable settings thronged by enthusiastic supporters are still *sine qua non* in campaigns, along with the harbingers who turn plans into realities. With enormous outlays for advertising, campaign salaries, travel, polling, and sophisticated technologies, it is no wonder that money has come to rule presidential campaigns.

However, the role of money was not nearly as central in the 1964 presidential campaign, the period most frequently addressed here. The advance in what had become Lyndon Johnson's campaign was modestly staffed and supported. Although the outcome of the campaign, LBJ's election, should have been clear from the beginning, the harbingers out front certainly contributed to the landslide. Their role, though, was never publicly acknowledged or understood. Johnson's penchant for secrecy was a major reason. In what most people would consider an ordinary communication, LBJ could see a traitorous "leak." He told his advance men to remain anonymous and keep their mouths closed. They did.

With the year 1963 expiring, President John Fitzgerald Kennedy and his advisers had begun planning for the campaign in the following year to keep him in the White House for a second term. This was the signal for Jerry Bruno, JFK's feisty chief advance man, to start looking for advance men to precede the president on his campaign trips. Aggressive advance preparations were a hallmark of Kennedy-style campaigning. Bruno and his boss, presidential appointments secretary Kenny (for Kenneth P.) O'Donnell, wanted experienced, or at least savvy and prudent, forerunners to make the arrangements for campaign "stops" in 1964.

A pre-campaign, five-city trip to Texas by the president and his Texan running mate, Vice President Lyndon Baines Johnson, was an early starting point. Much of the itinerary for the late November trip was advertised as nonpolitical, but the motivating purposes, of course, were to attract campaign contributions and gain voting support in a state that had barely endorsed the Kennedy-Johnson ticket in 1960.

A side benefit would be the multiple opportunities to test potential advance men for the '64 campaign. Among the likely sources for recruitment were federal agencies with political appointees who could be expected to possess party enthusiasm if not extensive experience in campaigns. They would be available, conveniently, in the pre-campaign period for assisting on nonpartisan presidential trips without having to resign from the government. If enlisted for the campaign, they would have to resign from the government, at least for that period.

I fit into the "likely" category. Bruno talked to Bernard L. Boutin, the New Hampshireman who was administrator of the General Services Administration (GSA), the federal agency in which I held a public affairs job. Boutin then talked to me, and I talked to Bruno. I found myself—willingly—an apprentice advance man who could be borrowed by the White House for nonpolitical trips while also working at my regular job in GSA. Experience? Ten years as a UPI correspondent and a year as press secretary and political adviser to a Democratic governor of Maine. The governor I served, Clinton A. Clauson, died in office. The governorship passed to the president of the state senate, a Republican. Maine had no lieutenant governor. It was time for this Democrat to move on.

Through administration contacts, I was appointed to the GSA position in the spring of 1961. The Byrne family—myself, wife, and four sons born in Maine—moved to Washington. I was a minor but an enthusiastic New Frontiersman. A song, "I'm a Minor Federal Functionary," on which my sons and I collaborated one night and sang to the accompaniment of one son's guitar, did not understate my powers as deputy assistant administrator and director of information of GSA, the federal building and supply agency. I found the prospect of taking an active role in reelecting President Kennedy exciting and welcome.

A few explanatory words are in order about what some might consider peculiarities of this account. The reader will note that the first-person singular is often used in what, essentially, is a memoir. I subscribe to Henry David Thoreau's theory, the one expressed in his book about living by a lake in the woods, that an author should not fear the recurrent use of the "I" pronoun. As Thoreau put it:

> In most books, the I, or first person, is omitted; in this it will be retained. . . . We commonly do not remember that it is, after all, always the first person that is speaking. I should not talk so much about myself if there were anyone else whom I knew as well. . . . Moreover, I, on my side, require of every writer, first or last, a simple and sincere account of his own life, and not merely what he has heard of other men's lives.

Secondly, there are numerous digressions, just as there are in life. If the reader is to depend upon the eyes and ears of a narrator, then it seems reasonable to make available to him or her what is going on in the mind of the teller, if that can be ascertained. We all carry our beliefs and our pasts turtlelike as we go.

Thirdly, although I participated in performing a useful service for two presidents, I was a confidant of neither but situated as a witness of their activities at certain times.

Fourthly, although I am generally known by my nickname "Jeb," associates in the LBJ advance unit got in the habit of calling me by my given name, "John." Don't be confused. That's me too. Finally, although memory is the constant and understood "footnote" for the sourcing of this account, my recollections have been stimulated by the contents of two grocery cartons brought down from the attic, records in no discernible order. There were trip schedules in varying stages of development, stray notations of air distances and flying times, city maps, plane and helicopter manifests, tentative programs, final programs, lists of reception and departure committees, tickets, photographs, news clippings and tear sheets, memoranda, letters, reports, identified lists of names, mystifying lists of names, and odd scraps of paper bearing names. They were the detritus from many hotel and motel rooms. Following several sorting sessions, the papers were separated into file folders that were arranged chronologically. In the folder first in line, stapled to the first sheet, was a pasteboard ticket:

My first assignment as a presidential advance man was President Kennedy's last stop before Dallas.

CHAPTER 1

Breakfast Before Dallas

My unplanned interlude as a presidential advance man began early in September 1963 in Washington when I met with Jerry Bruno, President John Kennedy's chief advance man, to discuss whether I should sign on as a part-time advancer for presidential trips. We talked about my experience as a journalist and—later—as an aide to a Democratic governor of Maine. The question was whether my experience would qualify me as one of the advance men for JFK's upcoming trip to Texas.

We agreed that my credentials to handle arrangements for one of the five stops on the trip did not guarantee a perfect fit, but, on the other hand, they were not disqualifying. The next question was to which of the cities—San Antonio, Houston, Fort Worth, Dallas, or Austin—should I be sent. When Dallas was mentioned as a possibility, I recalled the difficulties that Adlai Stevenson and Texas's own Lyndon Johnson had experienced there from unruly right-wingers. I suggested that Dallas might not be the place for a novice at the advance man's game. By the end of the conversation, we agreed that I would go to Fort Worth, the old cow town turned aircraft builder on the Trinity River, thirty miles west of Dallas.

Bruno's instructions were cryptic. He gave me some names: Bill Duncan, the Secret Service agent who would be in charge of security at Fort Worth; Raymond Buck, president of the Fort Worth Chamber of Commerce, which was sponsoring the local event, a breakfast, for the president; O. C. Yancey Jr., president of the Tarrant County AFL-CIO. He said that as soon as I arrived in Fort Worth I should find out how the tickets for the breakfast were to be distributed, how many the White House could have, and how many would be reserved for labor. I was to be sure that the breakfast was integrated. He handed me an onionskin copy of the Texas schedule, which began:

Nov. 21—Thurs.   Leave D.C. for San Antonio
                   3 hours 20 minutes flying time

The president's movements in San Antonio, Houston, Fort Worth, Dallas, and Austin were timed off in detail. I skipped to the Fort Worth entries, which began on Thursday night:

10 pm	Leave Houston 45 minutes flying time to Fort Worth
10:45 pm	Arrive Ft. Worth Carswell A.F.B. 20 minutes by car to Hotel Texas in downtown Ft. Worth
11:05 pm	Arrive Hotel Texas for night

I paused. Novice though I was, I would have the overnight stop. The schedule picked up on Friday, November 22:

8:45 am	Leave for Grand Ballroom in Hotel Texas Breakfast one hour
9:45 am	Leave breakfast for room
10:45 am	Depart hotel 20 minutes ride to Carswell A.F.B.
11:05 am	Arrive Carswell A.F.B.
11:15 am	Depart airport for Dallas

"What you do," said Bruno, "is get down there and keep in touch with us. We got to know everything that happens, everything you're doing. No plans should be made for the president. Check out things. I'll call you when there's a flight going down. Probably be about a week."

I went back to my office.

Bruno telephoned a few days later and told me when and where to catch the plane for Texas. He gave me another name, that of Fort Worth lawyer David O. Belew Jr., who was a contact with Governor John Connally.

"Be sure you talk with him," said Bruno.

Andrews Air Force Base lies to the south of Washington in its Maryland outskirts. It was there that I caught the plane. The date was November 12, 1963, the day after Veterans Day, or, as I continued to think of it in honor of what my family called Uncle Artie's war, Armistice Day. The plane had propellers and two engines. We would be a long time getting to Texas by jet-age standards. This was to be no luxury flight. After a lengthy wait at base operations, we boarded the aircraft, the "we" being, I gathered, advance men for the cities on the president's itinerary, Secret Service agents, and specialists from the White House Communications Agency. I knew no one on the plane, which took off and began to make slow progress toward the Southwest. I had brought nothing to read, so I dozed and mused and looked out the window at the American quilt. I thought of another November, not long before, when I had met Jack Kennedy.

It had been late in the afternoon of November 15, 1959, at the hilltop airport in Augusta, Maine. His hair blowing in the wind, Senator Kennedy came down the ramp from the family plane. Newspapermen were waiting to question him. But it was cold as well as windy, and the official greeting party had taken cover. So I told the senator that I was press secretary to his host, Maine Governor Clinton A. Clauson, and I suggested that he meet with the press at the Blaine House, the governor's mansion, where he was to go anyhow.

"Fine," he said, waving to the reporters. "I'll see you there."

He turned to me and pointed toward a heavyset figure coming off the plane. "Why don't you get together with Pierre?"

While Kennedy and others in his party rode in the governor's car to the former home of James G. Blaine, Maine's Republican "plumed knight," whose chances of winning the presidency had been diminished by a supporter's remark that the opposing party stood for "rum, Romanism, and rebellion," Pierre Salinger, Kennedy's press secretary, and I became acquainted as we rode down the airport hill in my station wagon. We talked about Maine politics and Jack Kennedy's possibilities of receiving timely Maine support for the Democratic presidential nomination. When we arrived at the Blaine House, Pierre asked me to look at the speech the senator was to deliver that evening at the Maine Democratic Party's Issues Conference being held at the Calumet Club, a Franco-American clubhouse, in Augusta. He wanted to know if I thought that Kennedy's prepared remarks in favor of the Passamaquoddy tidal power project were appropriate.

"Well, yeah," I said without enthusiasm. Most politicians working Maine got around to "Quoddy" sooner or later, the long-talked-of and never-built project to harness the huge tides of Passamaquoddy and Cobscook Bays between Maine and New Brunswick.

John Kennedy met the press sitting on a sofa in the glassed-in sunporch of the Blaine House. The questioning was brisk, and several of the reporters expressed admiration later for his knowledge and answers. One of them in his piece on the news conference made something of Kennedy's vest, considering it an attempt by the presidential aspirant to add maturity to his forty-two years. Kennedy and Salinger both appeared to appreciate the spirited questioning. Kennedy told us that it was a relief to face ranging, substantive questioning after coming from places where reporters never left the subject of his religion.

The hard politicking took place that night in a back room on the second floor of the Blaine House, where Kennedy, Connecticut Governor Abe Ribicoff, Connecticut State Democratic Chairman John Bailey, and others of the entourage met with Governor Clauson and the Democratic members of the Maine congressional delegation, Senator Edmund S. Muskie and Congressmen Frank M. Coffin and James C. Oliver. I was in and out of the room because the governor had a houseful of guests to meet John Kennedy, and I had many duties. The heart of the conversation was whether and when Maine's Democratic leadership would endorse Senator Kennedy's impending candidacy for the Democratic nomination for president. Governor Clauson had told me earlier in the day that, as far as he was concerned, "Sure we'll go for Kennedy, a New England man. We'll just have to decide when to do it." The governor that night appeared ready to issue an endorsement, but the congressional delegation seemed reluctant to take quick action. Senator Muskie, for one, had to consider that three of his Senate colleagues in addition to Kennedy would be in the race: Senators Symington, Humphrey, and Johnson.

The back room conversation over, not to the full satisfaction of the visitors, Senator Kennedy and his party flew back to Massachusetts. By the middle of December, the Maine Democratic leaders had agreed on an endorsement of Kennedy to be made public a few days after the formal announcement of his candidacy. Governor Clauson was to issue the joint statement on January 5, 1960, in the Maine State House. I issued it in his name with the approval of the Maine Democrats in Washington. The governor was dead. He had died in his sleep on December 30, 1959. Issuing the statement of support for Kennedy was my last act in the governor's office, where I had stayed on to pack up Governor Clauson's files. With no lieutenant governor, the Republican president of the state senate, John H. Reed, became governor. I moved over to the State Department of Economic Development and stayed on in Maine for another year, joining the Kennedy administration in Washington in the spring of 1961. More than two and a half years of minor federal functioning slipped by. Now, with President Kennedy preparing to seek reelection, I was on a plane to Texas. Looking out the plane window I recalled Thoreau's observation more than a century earlier when he questioned the haste with which the magnetic telegraph was being extended from Maine to Texas. "Maine and Texas, it may be, have nothing important to communicate." I wondered if times had changed.

As the plane droned on, I met some of my fellow travelers. Max Edwards, an experienced advance man, introduced himself and bought a drink. Later, a lithe and dark young man worked his way down the aisle, checking names left and right. Bill Duncan, the Secret Service agent assigned to Fort Worth, was looking for me. With him was another agent to be at Fort Worth, Ned Hall, a thin man with close-cropped hair. Duncan rounded up Major Jack Rubley, the communications officer for Fort Worth, and his assistant, Bill Harnett, a young lieutenant. We talked and sized up each other.

Fort Worth was the next-to-last stop. It was after 6 p.m., Texas time, when the plane landed at Carswell Air Force Base to discharge the Fort Worth contingent. An Air Force car met us and took us to the Hotel Texas, where we checked into our rooms and cleaned up after agreeing to meet for dinner. Joining us was Mike Howard, an agent from the Dallas Secret Service office, who was to work with Duncan and Hall. The six of us ate steaks in the Cattlemen's Restaurant and exchanged notes on our plans for the next day. Rubley and Harnett already had been in contact with the Southwestern Bell representative who would help them make the communications arrangements. They would be joining him in the morning. My plans were to see Raymond Buck. I had telephoned him from the hotel and arranged to be at his office early the next day, Wednesday, November 13. I suggested to Duncan and Hall that they accompany me so that all of us would know what planning had been done before our arrival. After dinner we drove around town to become familiar with the street patterns.

The next morning, I wondered for a moment if Buck manufactured shovels as a sideline. There was a row of them along a wall of his spacious, ground-floor offices. They were not, however, fated to gouge dirt and toss rock. Each of them, painted and bearing a plaque, had been used once in a groundbreaking ceremony for a new building.

Lawyer, president of insurance companies, and a past Democratic state chairman, Buck was a big man with white hair curling around the back of his neck.

"I'm the last of the long-haired Texas politicians since Tom Connally died," he told us as we sat around a conference table. This was a reference to a former senator from Texas, Thomas Connally (no relation to Governor Connally), who had died recently and whose Senate seat, which he had vacated in 1953, was held by Ralph Yarborough. Buck said that he had long been a friend of Lyndon Johnson's. Buck and I did the talking about the basic arrangements for the visit; the Secret Service agents listened. Some presidential advance men, I was to discover, maintained hostile relationships with the Secret Service, excluding agents from planning sessions in which security was not an obvious factor. From the start, however, I found the agents nonpolitical professionals. I made an effort to make sure that they knew what I knew. I hoped that they knew much more.

Buck said that he had been waiting for guidance from Washington, that little had been done yet on the presidential breakfast. The grand ballroom of the Hotel Texas had been reserved, but no invitations or tickets had been issued. The ballroom would hold 2,000 persons, including the working press, who would not be eating. The chamber of commerce planned to send out a letter to its members inviting them to apply for tickets. Buck said that there were about 3,000 members of the chamber, and he expected that at least 1,000 tickets would be requested, half for members and half for wives. Buck gave me a rundown on other requests for tickets: Governor Connally sought 200 to 300; Congressman Jim Wright of Fort Worth wanted 300 to 400; Senator Ralph Yarborough was expected to ask for a sizable number; labor, the Democratic county organization, and a state senator were seeking blocs of tickets; and there were tentative arrangements to set aside 50 for local federal officials, 50 for county officials, and 25 for city officials.

Visualizing the quick disappearance of all the tickets, I made haste to enter a White House claim for at least 200. Buck nodded. He said that the letter to chamber members would say that tickets would be limited, and that they would have to be picked up on a first-come, first-served basis. Members of the chamber were to pay $3 a ticket. Buck said that he and "several others" would pay for the rest.

When I raised the question of integration, Buck said he understood that about thirty of those attending on labor tickets would be blacks. Although he had indicated that little had been done about arrangements, a basic program had been laid out and a head table proposed, neither requiring many changes. The regular breakfast guests were to be served starting at 8 a.m. and would be through with their meals by the time the Kennedys arrived in the ballroom. A small orchestra and the Texas Boys' Choir were to perform. There would be a long head table to accommodate heads of local governments, vice presidents of the chamber of commerce, and a labor union representative, as well as the important personages from Washington and Austin. Wives, too. Buck, tactfully, had not scheduled himself to introduce the president, but I did so after talking with Bruno. The president was to speak starting at 9:10 a.m.

After leaving Buck's office, the Secret Service agents dropped me off at the hotel while they began to make their police contacts. I talked to Bruno, to my own office, to the GSA regional office in Dallas, and to David Belew, the Fort Worth attorney who was Governor Connally's contact. In the afternoon I went to Belew's office, where he explained that his wife Marjorie was a Democratic state committeewoman, and that because of her position both she and he were being badgered by people seeking information about the president's activities in Fort Worth. It was from Belew that I learned first that Democratic Party regulars were expressing indignation over the format of the president's visit, which seemed to them to be designed to keep the president away from rank-and-file Democrats. I agreed to go to the Belew home that night to talk with the Fort Worth couple, and others whom they would invite, about the difficulties posed by the visit as planned thus far.

The "others" at the Belew home, in addition to the pajama-clad Belew children, who ducked in and out of the living room, were Garrett Morris, Democratic state committeeman, who was introduced as campaign manager for Connally in the last campaign, Tarrant County Democratic Chairman William Potts, representatives of two unions—Garland Ham of the United Auto Workers and John Heath of the International Association of Machinists—and a public relations man who preferred to remain anonymous.

The group was unanimous in pressing for public exposure of the president while he was in Fort Worth. Proposals were made that

President Kennedy, in addition to his address at the breakfast, speak to a public gathering either in the parking lot across the street from the Hotel Texas, or four blocks from the hotel at Burnett Park, where he had spoken as a candidate in 1960, or at Carswell Air Force Base following the breakfast. I was a good listener.

In the following days it became obvious that those participating in the meeting at the Belews had assessed accurately the widespread dissatisfaction among Democrats. As my name and mission became known, my telephone in the Hotel Texas rang with more and more complaints. Labor leaders particularly were incensed by chamber of commerce sponsorship of the breakfast. I discussed with Buck the recommendations I had received for a public appearance of the president. Buck, who I am sure knew more than I did about the Washington-Austin agreement concerning the Fort Worth program, had no objection to any of the proposals as long as they did not affect the nonpartisanship of the breakfast to which he had been committed before I came to town. I passed along to Bruno the suggestions that I had received, a report on the extent of complaints, and my own recommendation that President Kennedy's schedule be revised to include a public appearance outside the hotel at which he would speak at least briefly.

I had been reading in the newspapers about the poor relationships between liberal Senator Ralph Yarborough and Texas's other leading Democrats, Vice President Johnson and Governor Connally, but I had taken for granted that the differences, which had risen to bitterness between the senator and governor, would be at least papered over while President Kennedy's pre-campaign Texas tour was in progress. I was startled, therefore, to begin to receive messages from Connally people that were clearly designed to give second-class treatment to Senator Yarborough.

First it was David Belew passing along the word from Scott Sayers, a Connally political operative in Austin, that the governor wanted this order for the motorcade in Fort Worth:

president's car
vice president's car
governor's car
press cars
Senator Yarborough's car

"Tell 'em," snapped Bruno on the telephone when I brought this up, "that the Secret Service takes care of motorcades."

Then came requests (or were they instructions?) from several directions, but with a common source in Austin that senators and congressmen should be seated at the breakfast on a dais lower than that for the president, vice president, and governor.

"Tell 'em," said Bruno, "that we follow protocol."

Bill Turner, exalted ruler of Fort Worth Lodge 124 of the Benevolent and Protective Order of Elks, appeared on the scene representing Senator Yarborough at this time to inform me that the senator had instructed him to see that protocol was "strictly followed" on the Fort Worth leg of the trip.

"If that means equal treatment," I told him, "the senator will get it."

Bill D. Moyers, then deputy director of the Peace Corps and a rising Johnson protégé, telephoned and began asking questions about the Fort Worth arrangements.

"How come?" I asked. Moyers said that he was in Austin and was serving as a coordinator for the trip. I said that I hadn't heard.

Bruno and I were beginning to have excitable conversations. When I told him about Moyers's call, he flared.

"What's he doing in this thing? You're the advance man there. We're running things here."

Later Bruno called me back. "About Moyers. It's okay. If he's got requests, fill 'em." Jerry had talked to someone.

Scott Sayers sent word that he was coming to Fort Worth and wanted to meet with me. We met. I was asked about the requests that I had received. I said that we would follow normal political protocol, meaning fair treatment. It was a short meeting.

The tempo of the final days accelerated. Demands for tickets became unceasing. Twelve hundred tickets were set aside for the chamber of commerce. Buck kept control of the rest. With his cooperation, I allocated and distributed 550 of the tickets, making them available principally to Democrats, union members, supporters of Senator Yarborough, blacks, and Chicanos. I required each group to compile lists of the names and addresses of intended recipients and to give them to me before I would make the tickets available. The executive vice president of the chamber, Milton Atkinson, who talked and acted like a conservative, became exasperated because so many of the tickets were straying from the chamber fold. We had words when I answered his complaint with the observation that there were other interests to be considered than those of the Fort Worth Chamber of Commerce.

While talking with a labor delegation in my room at the Hotel Texas, I became concerned about the extent of black attendance at the breakfast. One of the union leaders told me that despite what I might have heard about a substantial number of blacks being among the labor representatives at the breakfast, "there will be damn few unless somebody does something." I asked if anyone knew the number of blacks living in Tarrant County. When the union men told me there were 70,000, I asked for the name of a leader in the black community. Dr. Marion Brooks was suggested. As the labor delegation was going out the door, I was on the telephone with Dr. Brooks and with his assistance placed forty tickets directly with blacks.

With the Chicanos, I nearly struck out. The day before the breakfast the county sheriff telephoned and said that a young man on his staff by the name of Jake Cardenas headed the local Political Organization of Spanish-Speaking People (PASO) and was hurt that no one had made a move to involve the Chicanos in the presidential visit. I talked to Cardenas and apologized.

"I didn't think of it," I said.

He was polite, but his voice was numb. "Nobody does."

I was at the bottom of my ticket barrel but succeeded in retrieving ten tickets, which he picked up.

While I was engaged with my set of problems, Duncan and Hall, with an assist from Howard, went about their business of providing for the safety of the president while he was in Fort Worth. They met with law enforcement agencies that would be involved in the visit, checked the backgrounds of hotel employees and others who would be in contact with the presidential party, "ran out" and timed motorcade routes, including alternates, made arrangements for tight security on the president's quarters in the hotel, and went through the other rituals peculiar to their calling. We met at night to compare notes.

Mike Howard, the Secret Service agent later assigned by Duncan to be "law enforcement liaison," told me later that he called on Fort Worth Police Chief Cato Hightower to advise him of "what was about to fall on him." Howard sought the chief's help in reviewing records of people in the area who might be threats to the presidential party. Thirty people were detained or placed under surveillance, according

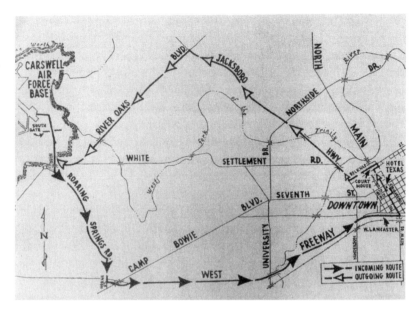

Fort Worth motorcade routes. *National Archives.*

to Howard. The agent asked Tarrant County Sheriff Lon Evans to contact all law enforcement agencies in the county and to tell them that every *body* was needed on November 21 and 22. The call was answered, and even firemen turned out to guard the hotel exits and stairwells.

Howard said that each floor and window in the tall building facing the parking lot where the president would speak on Friday was thoroughly checked, and the occupants were told to keep their windows shut on November 21 and 22. However, said Howard, on Thursday afternoon a policeman spotted an open window on an upper floor. It turned out, the agent said, that two teenage boys were looking at the activity in the parking lot through a scope attached to a hunting rifle belonging to their father, an attorney in the office. The gun, taken from an office gun case, was not loaded. It was determined that it was just innocent curiosity on the part of the boys, and the weapon and scope were locked away.

Howard also enforced a violation of the time in his agency's jurisdiction. An entrepreneur in the hotel lobby was selling $1 bills with the image of the presidential couple over George Washington's. He was shut down.

Ross Wilder, a big, hearty man who had been one of the pilots on Jimmy Doolittle's raid on Tokyo in World War II, came over from Dallas, where he was linked to my office in Washington as regional director of business affairs for the GSA. Ross introduced me to the owner of the Empire Club down the street where, after being signed on as a "member" in accordance with the quaint Texas custom of the time, I could buy hard liquor by the drink.

In addition to being sociable, I kept up an old habit of wandering alone in towns strange to me. On one of my walks I saw an interesting sale and emerged from a store wearing a Texas hat, trying to appear nonchalant under it, although usually I never wore a hat of any kind, much less one of Texas's hyperbolic headpieces. Twice I visited The Cellar, a below-the-street joint a few blocks from the hotel, where early hippie types congregated and weird concoctions, supposedly without alcohol, were served to the thrum of drums and guitars. In each instance my ears could bear the din for about half an hour.

The Secret Service agents and I went out to Carswell Air Force Base together for a meeting with the commanding officer, Brigadier General Howard W. Moore. He told us that because Carswell was a Strategic Air Command base, the public would not be able to enter for the president's arrival and departure. I argued that an exception should be made, that it was an unusual occasion, and that the people of the Fort Worth area should be able to see their president come and go. Carswell was opened to the public for the visit, but no doubt weightier voices than mine were responsible for the change in the original position that I had reported to Washington.

Inexperience as an advance man led to my being bullied by the Fort Worth labor leadership on one issue. I had made provision for Yancey and his wife to represent labor on the reception and departure committees. In the meeting with the labor leadership in my hotel room, Yancey and other officials of the Tarrant County AFL-CIO suddenly balked at this plan and threatened a labor boycott of the breakfast unless the other union county officials and their wives got to meet the Kennedys too. So an elongated reception committee greeted the presidential party on the night of November 21, and, as a departure committee, said goodbye on the morning of November 22. There was Raymond Buck and his wife, General Moore and his wife, the three vice presidents of the chamber and their wives, the chairman of the Tarrant County Democrats and his wife, the Democratic committeeman and committeewoman and their spouses, six officials of the Tarrant County AFL-CIO and their wives, the mayor and his wife, and the county judge and his wife. Later, one of my trademarks as an advance man was the compactness of reception and departure committees. But by then I had recognized that you can be firm when running the only presidential show in town.

The meeting with the union leadership also led to my discovery by the press. Following the session that had ended with me on the telephone to Dr. Brooks, the *Fort Worth Star Telegram* ran a front-page story headlined NEGROES INVITED TO BREAKFAST FOR JFK and crediting unnamed "organized labor spokesmen" with prodding "one of the White House aides at the Hotel Texas" into issuing invitations to black people. After this story appeared, reporters went hunting for the "aides" who turned out, of course, to be me. From then on I was quoted daily in the newspapers, saying vague things about plans for the presidential visit. As a rule, the prudent advance man tries to avoid getting his name into the newspapers. He lets local sources make the announcements. But sometimes the only choice is between candor and causing a disagreeable "tight-lipped mystery man at the hotel" news story.

Bill Turner, the exalted Elk, came to the hotel with a telegram that he had received from Washington after reporting to Senator Yarborough's office on our Fort Worth plans. Dated November 19, it read:

Seating, cars, head tables perfectly satisfactory.
Please do not object or complain, it is 100% perfect.
As to stopping at Elks lodge, will see what can be done.
Ralph Yarborough
U.S.S.

In addition to protecting Senator Yarborough's interests, Turner had been advancing one of his own, a visit to the Elks lodge by President Kennedy at which time the president would present an American flag to the lodge. Requests for presidents to make side excursions when visiting a community usually are legion. The majority are denied, as was this one. But Turner tried to the end. He sent long telegrams to Washington, and he kept after me by telephone and note, dignifying me with the written title "Special Assistant to the President and Member of the White House staff."

Congressman Jim Wright, young and personable, moved into the hotel a few rooms down the hall from mine and stayed on the telephone for two days. We did find time to discuss the Fort Worth planning and to deplore extraordinary examples of intra-party nastiness. Wright worked hard for White House approval of a public appearance by President Kennedy in addition to the breakfast speech. The day before the event, approval came through from Washington to schedule the extra remarks in the parking lot across the street from the Hotel Texas.

There had been another difficulty about the use of the parking lot as the site for early-morning remarks by the president before the breakfast address. Congressman Wright notes in his 1996 book *Balance of Power* (Turner Publications, 1996, p. 104) that he and Governor Connally had to work hard to convince oilman William A. Moncrief, who owned the city block that included the parking lot, that the lot could be used for the president's public appearance. Wright said that Moncrief, no Kennedy supporter, "finally relented."

Overall schedules of the Texas trip were appearing in the newspapers for the last few days before November 22. On November 19, a diagram was published in the Fort Worth newspapers of the routes that the president's motorcade would follow between Carswell Air Force Base and the Hotel Texas on November 21 and 22. High school bands agreed to play along the route. The Kennedy suite in the hotel was furnished with modern paintings and sculpture by local art lovers. Buck obtained through me the hat and shoe sizes of President Kennedy so that a Texas hat and a pair of boots could be presented to the president.

Ross Wilder came over from Dallas and moved into the hotel on November 21 to help me. There were three telephones in my room by this time, and the room rang like the inside of a campanile. Wilder and I ate a late dinner and then drove to Carswell, where Air Force One was to land shortly after 11 p.m. Streams of cars were entering the gates. As arrival time approached, I lined up the welcoming committee in a hangar and led the long column outside to the light-splashed apron. The blue-and-white 707 landed and taxied. The waiting crowd cheered as the aircraft marked with the American flag and the presidential seal cut its engines. The presidential party came down the steps and went through the receiving line. Marjorie Belew handed Mrs. Kennedy a dewy armful of three dozen red roses. The president and Mrs. Kennedy moved toward the fences. Cheers rose to a roar. Hands reached for theirs. There were laughter and shouts and a crescendo of cheers as they walked the fences, and, then, entered the cars. The motorcade began to move. Wilder and I got our car and headed for the Hotel Texas.

Downtown Fort Worth was alive with lights and people. We paused in the hotel lobby and talked to friends and acquaintances. Then I went up to the president's floor to report to Kenneth P. O'Donnell, the president's appointments secretary. O'Donnell was standing in the doorway of a suite laughing at the antics of David Powers, White House assistant and frequent companion of the president. Powers, in his shorts, was tumbling on the bed. O'Donnell looked at me.

"Why," he said, "did the congressmen have to wait at the desk in the lobby instead of being escorted to their rooms when the motorcade got here?"

I told him it was a detail that had not occurred to me. I must have looked abashed, because he followed up his abrupt greeting with, "Well, it's okay. Everything's fine."

We talked briefly about the next day's program, and I went back downstairs to Wilder's room where we were to have a drink with the owners of the Empire Club and his wife. Passing a hall mirror I realized that I was still wearing the Texas hat that I had put on to go to the airport. It occurred to me that a five-gallon hat was not the finest apparel for a Kennedy advance man to wear when talking with Kenny O'Donnell.

Looking back on the Fort Worth visit a year later, when I was a veteran at advance work, I recognized that the move of the presidential party into the old Hotel Texas that night was far from smooth, that I was not at the right places to plane the edges. With all the new problems I had been grappling with alone, I had slighted or ignored arrangements that later I would make as a matter of course. But the airport crowd had been good, the streets had been lined despite the late hour, and the presidential party was bedded down without any bad incidents. So on my way downstairs that night I was feeling good. I was tired, though, and anxious about the morning, so I declined an invitation to visit the Fort Worth Press Club, which was staying open late for the visiting newspapermen. Among those who did go were some off-duty Secret Service agents who had just arrived in town. After Dallas they were to be pilloried by Drew Pearson and others for drinking and keeping late hours while on a presidential trip. A few of the new arrivals visited The Cellar, the aforementioned nightspot. But there was no evidence of excessive drinking by Secret

Service personnel. As one agent told me, they were more interested in getting a bite to eat than a drink. Meals for agents on presidential trips could be haphazard. Following the nightcap with Wilder and his friends, I went to bed and left a call for early in the morning.

A drizzle was falling when I went out to the parking lot in the morning. On the roofs of buildings overlooking the lot, policemen in slickers stood against the gray sky. Despite the rain, the crowd swelled. The waiting people, many of them men in work clothes, were quiet. They watched the technicians adjusting the public address system on the flatbed that would serve as the president's platform.

President Kennedy, with Congressman Jim Wright by his side, strode out, neither of them wearing raincoats. Flanking them were Vice President Johnson and Senator Yarborough, with Governor Connally a few steps behind, all three protected against the drizzle by raincoats. It was 8:45 a.m.

"There are no faint hearts in Fort Worth," President Kennedy began when he had mounted the platform, "and I appreciate your being here this morning. Mrs. Kennedy is organizing herself. It takes longer, but, of course, she looks better than we do when she does it . . . we appreciate your welcome."

He went on to speak about the country's defense and the part that Fort Worth played industrially in maintaining the country's security. He touched on the nation's space effort. His words had an impromptu ring, but his delivery was warm and direct. He said that the people must be willing to bear the burdens of world leadership.

"I know one place where they are," he told his wet listeners. "Here in this rain, in Fort Worth, in Texas, in the United States. We are going forward."

There was prolonged applause from the 8,000 or so people in the parking lot. The president reentered the hotel. As prearranged, the breakfasters in the grand ballroom were on their coffee when the president, to vigorous applause, walked through the kitchen and down the aisle to the head table. I stayed in the kitchen doorway with a Secret Service agent. Mrs. Kennedy, lovely in a pink suit, came in behind us as Buck was introducing the head-table guests. She waited. He swung the attention of the audience to the kitchen entrance. Mrs. Kennedy stepped into the room to a tumultuous welcome. She went down the aisle to her husband amidst the wild cheering.

Buck presented the Texas hat and boots. President Kennedy thanked him and, to no one's surprise, did not put on the hat. He began his address lightly, referring to the frequent risings for applause during the introductions.

"I know why everyone in Texas, Fort Worth, is so thin, having gotten up and down about nine times. This is what you do every morning . . ."

The president's prepared remarks were directed to the country's defense posture. The parking lot talk had been a foretaste of what was to come. He enlarged upon Fort Worth's contributions to air defenses: World War II bombers, combat helicopters, the new TFX planes. It was a speech for a Texas chamber of commerce, and it was enthusiastically received. The president came up the aisle toward the kitchen with his wife. His young and vibrant face flashed smiles. Hands reached for him, and he grasped them. The Kennedys went into the kitchen and through a back door to the elevators.

As the crowd moved toward the exits, craggy Congressman Albert Thomas of Houston, whose big day had been Thursday in his own city, saw me and came over. Thomas, who was chairman of the subcommittee of the House of Representatives, which passed on the GSA's appropriations, shook my hand.

"Wonderful," he said. "Congratulations on what you fellows did here."

I felt a glow of architectonic accomplishment. Congressman Thomas had something in his other hand. He handed me a hat check and a quarter and asked if I would mind going through the crowd to get his hat on the other side of the ballroom, meeting him in front of the hotel where the motorcade cars were drawn up. He had missed his proper transportation once earlier in the trip and was determined not to do so again. A little deflated, I went after his hat. He need not have worried. The motorcade would not leave for another hour.

"Welcome Mr. President" read the lettering on the marquee of the hotel. The motorcade cars for the president and the vice president were parked at the curb. I stood to one side, arms folded, smoking, hopeful that the loading of cars would go smoothly but apprehensive that it would not.

Governor Connally and his wife emerged from the hotel. David and Marjorie Belew were on the sidewalk, and David introduced me to the governor. "I've heard about your work here in Fort Worth," Connally said suavely. "You did a good job I understand."

I thanked him. There was no mention of the unfulfilled requests from Austin.

Larry O'Brien was waiting nervously by the vice president's car. Ralph Yarborough had refused to ride with Lyndon Johnson in the other Texas cities on the previous day, prompting new press reports of their estrangement. O'Brien was charged with getting them both into the same car. Senator Yarborough was with O'Brien. Loosely. He wandered. O'Brien asked me in a low voice to seat the vice president in the rear of the car when he came out of the hotel. O'Brien muttered something like "You can do it easier than I can," and he said something further about his having to work with the vice president in Washington.

The automobile was a convertible with the top down. Yarborough entered the car but perched on the back of the rear seat on the driver's side. His occupancy seemed tentative.

A Secret Service agent came back from the president's car escorting Nellie Connally, the governor's wife. Without crowding, there was no room for her in the president's car, which was a five-passenger model, the same as the car assigned to the vice president. The president and Mrs. Kennedy and Governor Connally would ride in the rear seat of the president's car; the driver and another Secret Service agent would be in front, so there was no place for Mrs. Connally to go but the car behind. She was entering the rear seat of the vice president's car when O'Brien, his face working, moved in and plunked her into the middle of the front seat where she would ride between the driver and a Secret Service agent. O'Brien managed to keep a tether on Yarborough, who had been showing signs of relinquishing, with pleasure, his seat to this lady. Vice President and Mrs. Johnson came up to the motorcade. O'Brien stepped back, and I stepped forward.

"Here is your seat, Mr. Johnson," I said cheerfully, swinging open the rear door. He stared at me without comment as he struggled into a coat held for him by agent Rufus Youngblood. Mrs. Johnson slid into the middle of the seat next to Yarborough. The vice president climbed in. I shut the door. The deed was done. I quickly wondered how this motorcade episode would go down with the press. It would probably be somewhere up front in accounts of the morning events. The running story had been the split in the Texas Democratic Party. Typical had been the final paragraph in a piece in the November 18 *Dallas Morning News* before the trip had begun. Robert E. Baskin of the paper's Washington bureau had written: "The President's attitude toward Yarborough and other Texas party leaders will be closely watched during his visit." The close watchers, of course, would be reporters. Oh well, I thought, time will tell. But time did not. The incident became inconsequential as the day unfolded.

Up ahead, the Kennedys and Governor Connally settled into their white convertible which, Agent Howard recalls, had been borrowed by the Secret Service from professional golfer Ben Hogan. There were waves and cheers from the onlookers. The motorcade to Carswell began. Riding in a Secret Service car, Howard was pleased to see Tarrant County's "Mounted Posse" out in force to supplement police on foot. Rain had cancelled the planned presence of these deputies on horseback along the incoming route the night before. There was, Howard notes, an unscheduled stop by the presidential cavalcade along the way in the northwest suburb of River Oaks, the line of cars pausing while the president spoke to some nuns and a group of schoolchildren.

Ross Wilder, my helper from GSA's Dallas office, and I drove to Carswell by a different route to arrive at the air base before the motorcade did. The departure committee, formerly the welcoming committee, was already in place at my request. It did its duty. Thousands of people behind the barricades raised their voices as the big blue-and-white jet roared and began to roll. The plane took off at about 11:20 a.m., Texas time, for the flight to Love Field in Dallas, a little more than ten minutes away. Members of the serpentine departure committee, their faces warmly smiling, came up to me and shook my hand.

We drove back to the Hotel Texas, and I made a reservation on a commercial flight to Friendship Airport in Baltimore. Bruno telephoned from Washington and Moyers from Austin to ask how the morning had gone. After talking with them, I sat down at my portable typewriter and wrote a one-page final report on the Fort Worth leg of the trip. Then I lay down on the bed for a short nap. There was a furious knocking on the door. "Turn on your radio," Ross Wilder shouted. "Your boss is dead. Turn on your radio."

I switched on the hotel radio and let him in. Bulletin followed bulletin. A voice said that two priests emerging from a Dallas hospital room had confirmed that President Kennedy was dead. I turned off the radio. Wilder left. I lay on the bed and wept.

Wilder drove me to Love Field in Dallas to catch my flight, which I had cancelled and then rescheduled. I had a middle seat in the plane. My sobs would not stop, so I said to the men on either side, "You will have to put up with this. I was in Texas for the president."

From Baltimore I took the airport bus to Washington and a taxicab to my home south of Alexandria, Virginia. My wife, our four boys, and I stayed home in the days that followed.

After the federal city returned to work, I found myself still tied to the Texas tragedy. President Johnson named his commission to investigate the assassination. While the GSA sought suitable office space for the panel headed by Chief Justice Earl Warren, its members met in a conference room of the National Archives, then a part of the GSA. By agreement of the chief justice and the archivist of the United States, Wayne C. Grover, I accredited the reporters who converged on the archives building for the Warren Commission's first three meetings, and I served as press aide. Following the third meeting, the commission had a staff and offices in another building. My services ended.

Back in my own office, I was talking on the telephone one day to Wilder in Dallas and he said, "Do you remember Jack Ruby?"

"Yeah," I said, "I remember."

Henry Levy, a member of our staff, and I had been in Dallas months before the assassination of President Kennedy. When we had completed our business in the GSA regional office, we went to dinner with Wilder, and afterward somebody said, "How about a nightclub?"

Wilder asked the bartender in the restaurant, an old acquaintance, where we should go.

"Hold a minute," said the bartender, "let me call a guy."

When he hung up, he said, "Go to the Carousel. The guy says since I'm sending you, forget the door charge."

It was a walkup. A fat, balding man met us at the entrance and showed us to a table. Most of the tables were empty. It was Jack Ruby, who was to gun down Lee Harvey Oswald in the corridor of the police station. He stayed for a few minutes to tell us how good the show was. The MC came out on the stage, grabbing for a support. He was drunk. The decorations were shoddy, the drinks terrible. There was a laboring stripper. We paid up and got out.

"Goin' so soon?" said Ruby as we passed him.

In the weeks that followed close on November 22, 1963, it was difficult to realize that the Kennedy years were over. A sense of finality came to Washington on December 22 during the candlelight ceremony at the Lincoln Memorial that ended the thirty days of official mourning. The Howard University choir sang, the army band played, and clergymen prayed. It was bitter cold. The new president spoke, paraphrasing the words of Lincoln at Gettysburg. We lit candles, sang "America the Beautiful," and looked across the Potomac to Arlington National Cemetery, where there was another glint in the night, a reminder that in the short years before Dallas, hope had come to some arid places in America.

CHAPTER 2

Twitches on the Johnson String

My days as a presidential advance man, I assumed, were over. The president whom I had served so briefly in that capacity, whose administration I had come to Washington to join, was dead. New faces began to appear in the White House and the Executive Office Building. There were more Texas hats. Mine lay wadded in the corner of a closet shelf where I had hurled it while emptying my bag on the night of November 22. I do not know if all the instruments agreed, but that was a dark cold winter.

In the spring, Bill Moyers called me at home one night. We had never met, but he recalled our telephone association in Texas. Now, early in May 1964, he was speaking from the White House as a key Johnson assistant. The president was to leave Washington on a tour of Appalachia to dramatize its poverty. Would I take one of the stops? I agreed to. Wilson McCarthy, a Peace Corps associate of Moyers, came on the line with him. McCarthy was overseeing the advance for Moyers. I was to catch a commercial flight to North Carolina and meet Jerry Bruno and the Secret Service at Rocky Mount. The president would fly into Seymour Johnson Air Force Base in Goldsboro on May 7, helicopter to Rocky Mount where he would speak at the City Hall and visit a tenant farm, then helicopter back to Air Force One at Goldsboro. I was to handle the arrival and departure at Seymour Johnson. Okay? Okay.

Bruno and the Secret Service were ensconced in a motel in Rocky Mount when I arrived. I left soon by car with two of the agents for Goldsboro about forty miles south and took up residence in the Visiting Officers Club at Seymour Johnson. My part of the action during the president's two-day, five-state trip through Appalachia would be simple. Air Force One would set down at Seymour Johnson at about 5:30 p.m. on May 7, which was a Thursday. The president and those accompanying him, including members of the congressional delegation from the states on the tour, would switch to helicopters and fly up to Rocky Mount for about two hours, return to the air base to reboard their plane, and take off for Atlanta. So all I had to do was see to it that a crowd turned out for the arrival and hope that part of it would remain for the departure. If a large enough crowd could be assured, then the president would speak from a stand-up microphone upon arrival.

Counting on a crowd at an airfield where a president is changing aircraft can be risky from the advance man's standpoint. There are wide open spaces that swallow a modest crowd. The point of the exercise is not to make the president look lonesome. When a crowd is doubtful, onlookers sometimes are pointedly discouraged. The word is passed that the switch will take place on a remote part of the field, away from public areas. But this was not necessary at Seymour Johnson. As the *Goldsboro News-Argus* was to remind its readers on May 6:

> Johnson's visit here will be the first time a president has been to Goldsboro since Grover Cleveland came through on a train. It will be the first time a president has ever made an address here.

As an argument between nineteenth-century governors of North Carolina and South Carolina is said to have been brought to a close with the memorable observation of one of them that "it's been a long time between drinks," it was a long time between presidential presences in Goldsboro.

Well before the newspaper had been able to report that the president would speak at Seymour Johnson, I had become convinced that a sizable crowd would turn out and had so indicated to Washington. Governor Terry Sanford of North Carolina had sent an able aide, Charles Cohoon, to Goldsboro, and Cohoon was working with a local committee when I arrived. Cohoon, I, and the committee got along well, and the military cooperated, although there was one bird colonel, not one of the commanding officers, who became sarcastic when I inquired if directives had gone out making it possible for base employees to see their president. He interpreted the presidential visit as an affront to Barry Goldwater, who was pursuing the Republican nomination for president.

By the time Wilson McCarthy came flying in on a survey of the route, the Seymour Johnson stop was in good shape, and we were able to decide where to run the ropes and place the microphone. That was my first sight of McCarthy, a sleek, black-haired young man who did congressional liaison for the Peace Corps when it was a high art under Sargent Shriver. After looking over the planning at the air base, McCarthy suggested that I fly to Rocky Mount with him to see how things were going in that part of the operation. We rode a C-123 to Rocky Mount, a sort of flying boiler room. On the ground we caravanned around in cars with Secret Service agents and communications specialists, looking at the speech site and at the grim tenant farm that had been selected for the president to visit. McCarthy and Bruno did the gesticulating back and forth on this one; I just went along and watched and flew back to Goldsboro with McCarthy in the airborne boiler room.

When Air Force One landed at Seymour Johnson on May 7, the crowd was larger than I had anticipated. President Johnson went eagerly to the microphone.

"If you ever need pepping up a little bit in Washington," he said ebulliently, "all you have to do is get on the plane and go out and see the people. They are the optimistic group. Any of you that happens to be here when I return, I will be glad to have another little visit with you." He introduced his daughter, Lynda Bird, who was accompanying him, praised the North Carolina governor and congressional delegation, introduced some Washington officialdom, and walked the ropes for five minutes of handshaking after promising to be back "as soon as the sun lets down."

The North Carolina visit was off to a good start. But there was one unplanned incident. Two days earlier I had gone with one of the Secret Service agents to the base hospital where we lunched with the doctor who was in charge. We arranged for him to stand by with an ambulance, a usual precaution, when the presidential plane landed. After Air Force One did set down, I rallied many of the disembarked congressmen in a hangar and prepared to lead them to the fat C-123 to fly to Rocky Mount. The congressional contingent was a large one, and there were not enough helicopters for all.

The door through which I tried to lead them was one of those hangar doors that trace their ancestry to windows. The opening started a foot above the floor and did not rise very high. I was half turned to the file of congressmen and moving at a fast pace when my head struck the top of the doorway. Whap! I fell through the opening.

The doctor picked me up on the edge of unconsciousness. After he quickly patched my head, he said that we had shown prescience in having him park his ambulance four feet from the spot where I hit the ground. Dazedly, I continued on to the C-123.

Johnson visited the tenant farm in Rocky Mount and spoke both inside and outside City Hall. I heard later that there was a problem with the tenant farm visit in Rocky Mount. The farm had been chosen because of its visible evidence of Appalachian poverty. But between the advance inspection and the president's visit, the family and neighbors had spiffed up the place because of the impending visit of the president.

The schedule was running late, the presidential party returning to Seymour Johnson three hours after it had left. A good crowd was waiting, although it was after 9 p.m. Again the president strode delightedly to the microphone. He had his promised "little visit" with those who had stayed to watch his departure. On the flight to Atlanta, I was to hear later, the size of the crowd at Goldsboro received enthusiastic mention. I found myself on the Johnson string.

The string twitched in less than two weeks. Max Edwards, whom I had met on the flight to Texas, and I were dispatched to Roanoke, Virginia, where Air Force One would take the president on May 23. The George C. Marshall Research Library at Virginia Military Institute (VMI) in nearby Lexington was to be dedicated on that date. Presidents Eisenhower and Truman also were to attend, but the latter was compelled to cancel his plans because of illness. Edwards and I went about the business of arranging an airport stop at Roanoke's Woodrum Field. I drove over to VMI with the Secret Service to reconnoiter the program there. It was cut and dried and the military circumambiences too confining. So I returned to Roanoke, and we concentrated on the airport stop.

On the appointed day, President Johnson emerged from his plane at Roanoke with past and present Cabinet members, Senator Harry F. Byrd, other members of the Virginia congressional delegation, and various people who had been associated with General Marshall. Johnson jollied Senator Byrd at the microphone, introduced his fellow travelers, and looked hungrily at the massed Virginians.

"Thank you so much for coming out. We will have a chance to come by the fence and say hello to you." He went to the barrier and began clasping hands. Another tall figure who had arrived in the plane, elegant in brown from shoes to homburg, stood to the side on the sunny concrete apron. Dean Acheson moodily watched the president work the fences.

At Lexington there were many speeches under a hot sun. The next twitch had livelier consequences. Wilson McCarthy, a habitual late-night caller, reached me at home. The president was to speak at the United States Coast Guard Academy commencement in New London, Connecticut, on June 3. Would I fly up there?

McCarthy had a title to bestow.

"You," he said, "will be team captain." This was an honor I had not enjoyed since I played left field for the Iona Prep School baseball team in New Rochelle, New York, in 1943. The team I was to captain on this occasion was to be composed of two other advance men and several players with additional allegiances, Secret Service agents and communications specialists.

There was a possibility, McCarthy indicated, that a second speaking engagement for the president might be arranged at Groton, across the Thames River from New London, where nuclear submarines were built in General Dynamic's Electric Boat Company shipyard. Connecticut Senator Thomas J. Dodd was up for reelection, and his old friend from the Senate was willing to linger. Possibly it would help them both with the Connecticut electorate.

Ernest Ollson, the Secret Service agent in charge of security for the trip, had set up housekeeping at the Groton Motor Inn, so it was there that I and the two other advance men, Jack Howard and Ed Fecteau, took rooms. While we were establishing ourselves and eating the local bay scallops at a shore restaurant, The Lighthouse, word came through that we should start making arrangements for the additional speech in the submarine shipyard. That would mean, besides, that we could have a motorcade through both towns. I asked Fecteau to see what he could do about turning out the area's schools for the motorcade and arranging for high school bands to play. He was successful on both counts. His sign instigation program, though, ran into a hitch. A folksy, sidebar story in the June 2 edition of New London's newspaper *The Day* reported that

> An aide pointed out to one principal that it might be nice if the kids carried signs. The schoolmaster thought it would be fine too, except, some of the young'uns around here are for Goldwater. "Oh no," the principal was told, "this is non-political."

The same newspaper speculated on page one of that edition that 20,000 to 50,000 persons would view the motorcade but included this disclaimer:

> The police say they have no way to figure out the number in advance.

Lottery players have long been plagued with a similar problem.

The people at Electric Boat were eager to have the president lay the keel of the new nuclear attack submarine *Pargo* while he was in their shipyard. I experienced difficulty, however, in obtaining clearance from the White House. My instructions had been to place the speaking platform under a roofed-in part of the yard in case of rain. If the keel ceremony were to take place, then it would necessarily be down on the ways where President Truman had laid the keel for the first nuclear submarine, the *Nautilus*, in 1952. For a couple of days the answer to my telephone calls to Washington was "We're checking it out."

Finally, on June 1, approval came through, and I was able to pass the word to the shipyard officials who had numerous preparations to make.

I wrote a news release covering the New London-Groton events and had it reproduced along with a map of the motorcade route upon which we had decided. That afternoon, I met with reporters in the shipyard offices, distributed the prepared materials, and answered questions.

Howard's crowd-building activities were proceeding well, and state Democratic headquarters in Hartford was contacting the party faithful. This was the home state of John Bailey, chairman of the Democratic National Committee, and he was anxious that Connecticut turn out for the president.

June 3 was a beautiful day. Jones Field at the Coast Guard Academy where the commencement exercises were held lay bright green and close clipped in the sun. The program ran smoothly, the car assignments worked, and the motorcade wound through thick crowds interspersed with brassy bands. There were frequent stops while the president left his car to grab hands. I had provided the lead car with a map of the route, with expected crowd concentrations marked on it. At the shipyard, company officials briefed the president.

"What shall we brief him about," one of them had asked me when the White House put this requirement on the agenda.

"Submarines," I said.

At the waterfront I failed to recognize and halted one man with his head down who was ascending the speakers' platform. He raised his head.

"I am Senator Dodd."

"Certainly," I said. "This way, please."

The president burned his brand into the keel, in reality just writing his "LBJ" and letting a welder make the initials permanent.

"I declare the keel of the submarine *Pargo* well and truly laid," said the president. Then he talked about submarines and missiles. As usual, he made laudatory mention of the congressional delegation. Senators Dodd and Ribicoff were "my longtime friends" and "my two good and old friends." And it was "your own very able Congressman Bill St. Onge" and "your own fine Congressman Bill St. Onge." I was watching the face of the congressman whom I had come to know in the past few days. He winced each time he was mentioned. His name was pronounced "Onj," not "On'-jee" as the president said it. Perhaps his constituents might suspect that he was not as close to the president as Johnson seemed to imply.

The shipyard workers gave the president a hearty send-off. The motorcade rolled down the street to a field where we had moved the helicopters from their first landing place at the Coast Guard Academy. The presidential party departed for Air Force One, which had been left at Quonset Naval Air Station in Rhode Island. And we went back to Washington.

If President Johnson's first 1964 foray into New England had been encouraging, then his June 19–20 welcome to California must have convinced him that election to a presidential term on his own in November was a foregone conclusion. He drew enormous crowds in San Francisco and Los Angeles. The *San Francisco Chronicle* and the *San Francisco Examiner* reported that 500,000 people turned out in downtown San Francisco on June 19 to greet the president. The *San Francisco Chronicle* said he rode into "a forest of people the greatest crowds here since V-J Day." The *Examiner* said that he was the twelfth president to visit San Francisco while in office, and that his reception "was the most tumultuous of them all." These reports appeared on the day following his triumphant arrival. Some preparations had been made beforehand.

In Wilson McCarthy's athletic prose, I was the team captain for the San Francisco advance. With me again was Howard, who knew the area intimately and had been a labor reporter for the *Chronicle*. Chester Smith, who worked on the Senate side of the Capitol, was the other advance man. We had three major events to cover. In the morning the president was to take part in the ground breaking for the San Francisco Area Transit test track at Concord on the east side of the Bay. Then he was to dedicate the new federal building on Golden Gate Avenue in downtown San Francisco. The president was to end the day with an address at a Democratic fund-raising dinner at the San Francisco Hilton Hotel, which would be preceded by two cocktail parties, one at the Fairmount Hotel for the President's Club of large contributors and the second at the Hilton. The presidential party would spend the night at the Fairmount. I asked Howard to take the Concord program and Smith to work on the dinner and cocktail parties. I would handle the dedication of the federal building and the overall arrangements. The building dedication posed no special problems, because my office in the GSA ran such ceremonies as a matter of course, working through the appropriate field officials. The GSA regional office already had worked up a program at the federal building site according to our usual pattern, which merely had to be adapted for the president's participation.

The president was to fly into San Francisco International Airport in the morning, helicopter over to Concord, helicopter back to the airport after the transit program, and motorcade up the freeway to Main Street, where he would switch from a closed car to a top-down convertible and travel across Market Street to the federal building. After the dedication he would go to the Fairmount, attend the cocktail parties late in the day, and speak at the dinner that night.

The key decision was to shape the schedule so that the motorcade came down Market Street, San Francisco's principal thoroughfare, at the noon hour. Other moves to assure crowds were minor in comparison to that simple scheduling maneuver. But we made them anyway. Officials of the city, state, and chamber of commerce were requested to arrange for the release of employees at the proper time to see the president. Party and union officials were asked to concentrate their members at several places along Market Street. But contrivances proved unnecessary. The hour and what appeared to be a genuine desire on the part of San Franciscans to turn out for President Lyndon Johnson proved sufficient. The crowds were huge.

This was a stop where it was possible for Washington advance men to keep out of the newspapers. The Democratic State Central Committee, an efficient operation, issued the schedule and other information about the visit and also provided skilled volunteer help to handle many of the routine details that the advance men had supervised personally in New London.

Pierre Salinger, who had resigned from the White House staff and then defeated California State Controller Alan Cranston for the Democratic nomination for U.S. senator, was in the Fairmount making his own advance arrangements for the visit. He asked me if I would make sure that he got on Air Force One for the flight from Edwards Air Force Base into San Francisco. I called Washington. When I received approval I rang Salinger's room early in the morning to give him the news. He answered the telephone sleepily.

"Everybody got me on that plane," he said. "You're the fourth person to call."

At Concord, on June 19, President Johnson shook every hand he could reach, delivered his address, and pushed the plunger touching off a small charge of dynamite that signified the start of the transit project. A few minutes later the cheers of the crowd turned to shouts of outrage when the presidential helicopter whipped directly overhead at a low altitude, its blades kicking up a dust-and-paper storm. As the dust settled, however, tempers cooled, and the poor judgment of the pilot was forgotten.

The Concord excursion completed, the presidential party changed from helicopters to automobiles at the San Francisco airport and headed north on the freeway. Market Street was solidly and thickly lined when the motorcade swung into it, and the windows of the buildings were packed with people. Smiling broadly, the president climbed from his car three times to shake hands as the motorcade wound through the narrow lane formed by people spilling into the street. When he reached the federal building, the president directed that barriers be removed so that the crowd packed into the federal plaza could stand closer to the speakers' platform.

Near the end of his address, Johnson leaned toward the crowd and said emotionally:

I want to thank all of you for coming and giving us this warm welcome. I will always remember this visit to San Francisco. As a matter of fact, you make me feel so good that if I get distressed at all between now and next November, I think I am going to invite myself back to San Francisco.

Then he presented a replica of the Great Seal of the United States to Mayor John F. Shelley, a miniature of the large replica mounted on the building. This was an unscheduled touch. I had slipped a paper to Jack Valenti at the airport requesting the presentation and supplying the extra words. I could not have the president ignore the proper GSA dedication procedure that I had written for such occasions.

The cocktail party in the Crown Room of the Fairmount Hotel was one of those embarrassing affairs where the big contributors and their wives, dressed to kill, sit around stiffly and wait for someone to introduce the president to them. They paid $1,000 for the privilege. I went up and sampled the booze, which was good. Most things about the Fairmount Hotel, the gracious old hostelry atop Nob Hill, were good. I became one of the Fairmount's admirers. Richard Swig, the general manager, went the extra mile for a presidential visit.

Back in my hotel room I scribbled some silly verses about cocktail parties, the abominations of the Western world:

Cocktails

Tick
Tick talk
Tick talk tick talk
Tickety tickety tickety talk
Tickety talk
A tick a talk a tick a talk
A tickety tickety tick a talk
A talk a tick a talk a tick
Tickety tick talkety talk
A tick a talk a tick a talk
A tick a talk
Tick a talk
Tick talk
Tick
$1,000 please

If the second cocktail party at the Hilton Hotel materialized, I did not get to it. I went over in time for the dinner. There were picketers marching in circles on one side of the hotel. Ironically, on this night when the Senate back in Washington was passing the Kennedy-

Johnson civil rights bill, many of those picketing the president were civil rights activists. Their signs indicated that they wanted him to intervene in San Francisco trials in which civil rights were involved. Other picketers protested the U.S. involvement in Vietnam. Some chanted "Hey, hey, what d'yu say, let's get rid of the CIA." When the picketing plans had been announced, California's Democratic leaders had condemned them, but that did not deter the picketers.

At the Hilton, the Democratic diners learned that Senator Edward Kennedy had been seriously injured in an airplane crash. There was no announcement. The news circulated, causing apprehension. Eventually word was passed that the youngest brother of John Kennedy would survive.

Governor Edmund G. (Pat) Brown, in his remarks, revised his pre-primary estimate of Pierre Salinger as a "rookie" by saying that he had turned out to be "Rookie of the Year." Salinger, a lively campaigner, had been in the center of activity all day long.

Long afterward, President Johnson was to disclose that he did not make up his mind whether or not he would seek the presidency on his own until the Democratic National Convention was meeting in Atlantic City in August. This night in California, however, he did not appear to have any reservations. He said that he was seeking a job, and he told the California Democrats "I hope you love me in November as you do in June."

The next morning I indulged myself. I climbed into the lead police car of the motorcade and rode to the airport, looking back from time to time at the squadrons of red-lighted motorcycles and the column of black cars as we sped down the freeway.

After Air Force One had departed for Southern California, I returned to the city and took a last ride on a cable car. Then I checked out of the hotel and headed for Washington.

CHAPTER 3

Mission Anonymous

When the tide went out at Popham Beach in Maine, it went far out. If you had a mind to, then you could walk to Wood or Fox Islands when the waters withdrew. If you did not have a mind to, then you could lie on the strand of a summer's day and think long thoughts. Early in August 1964, I rose from the sand and, with a barrel stave thrown up by the ocean, wrote in large letters on a long strip of beach lately covered with water

> 'My name is Ozymandias, king of kings:
> Look on my works, ye Mighty, and despair!'

Then I lay down again to watch the tide come in.

It is a free country, and sometimes you can spend your vacation the way you want to. My wife and I had decided that it was time for us to return with our four boys to refresh ourselves in Maine. We knew Popham Beach of old, lying just west of the mouth of the Kennebec River. A band of would-be colonists under George Popham tried to settle this tip of the Sagadahoc peninsula in 1607, which would have given them a running start on the sturdies who were yet to land at Plymouth Bay to the south. But after one Maine winter, the Popham company—what was left of it—sailed back to England.

We were staying in a small house crouched behind the dunes, which we had not noticed in earlier years, or, if we had, probably thought it an outbuilding to one of the neighboring Victorian houses that lifted their fretwork high. One evening when we were at soup, Mr. Spinney, who ran Spinney's store and restaurant and a few rooms and a few cabins, knocked at the back door and told us that my office in Washington had telephoned the store and that the woman caller was anxious that I call back early the next day.

I telephoned Dorothy Knox, my secretary, from Spinney's in the morning, and she said that Wilson McCarthy had called, wanting to speak to me in the worst way and asking if she could find me. So I called Wilson, and his husky voice came on the line.

"John," he said, "we need you to help run the advance team for the president. You'll have to resign from the government because the president will be a candidate, but later you will be able to name your job."

I hemmed and hawed a little about family responsibilities but came around to saying "probably," and we agreed that I would go to his office in a few days when we returned to Washington. Our vacation time was running out.

After we had driven our station wagon back to Washington filled with gritty boys and shells, I went calling on McCarthy at the Peace Corps. Marty Underwood, an old hand as an advance man who had handled Houston on John Kennedy's Texas trip and who was at the Department of Commerce, came in. The way McCarthy explained the situation to us was that he would have the day-to-day responsibility for advance arrangements for the president's trips during the campaign, under the direction of Bill Moyers. Underwood and I would be McCarthy's deputies.

"I want you two to be able to speak for me and sign for me," McCarthy said. "We will be on the road a lot, but one of us should be in the office at all times." The three of us would be resigning from the government to take part in the campaign. Also to quit the government were McCarthy's secretary, Peggy Stark, and a young assistant, Harold Pachios, and another Peace Corps associate, Padraic (Pat) Kennedy. Our office would be located in the headquarters of the Democratic National Committee, then at 1730 K Street. Mel Cottone of the DNC joined us. Our first advance would be the Democratic National Convention in Atlantic City, New Jersey, where LBJ would be nominated for his own term as president.

Sometime in the hurly-burly of the preparations for the start of the campaign, there was a meeting at the White House in the mess—an eating place, not a confirmation of Republican accusations—in the West Wing. Moyers called the meeting of those who were expected to be advance men in the months ahead. He had notified me that I would be one of the experienced advance men called upon to talk about running an advance operation. I was on my feet making a point about the usefulness to advance men of teletyped plane and helicopter manifests when there was a commotion in the corridor. In strode the president. I sat down. President Johnson began by saying that Moyers would be in charge of advance arrangements. The rest of the meeting was described accurately by Drew Pearson's post-election column printed in *The Washington Post*, and presumably other newspapers, on November 8. (See page vi for Pearson's report explaining why LBJ's advance men were "anonymous.")

We resigned from the federal service and looked over space in the offices of the Democratic National Committee. There were some commodious bullpen areas to choose from, but McCarthy had his eye on a room that, although cramped for our operation, had doors to shut. He picked a desk and hung an oil portrait of Ernest Hemingway, the Hemingway of the gray stubble, on the wall behind him. But there was no time for settling in. August was in its second half, and the first campaign advance was beckoning: the Democratic National Convention in Atlantic City, New Jersey, August, 25–28. Time to arise and go there.

Page Airways was running a Democratic shuttle from Washington to Atlantic City. I caught a morning flight and on the other end put my bag into a room reserved for Underwood and me in the garish Galaxie Motel, which was a few blocks from the convention hall. Marty was not around, so I sauntered down to the convention hall into a world of confusion. The convention offices were upstairs, that of convention Executive Director Leonard Reinsch on one side of the hall, that of LBJ's Texas overseer, Marvin Watson, directly opposite. Revealing. I called upon each. Then, equipped with an "all areas" pass hanging from my neck on a clear plastic cord and a radio buzzer resembling a black kazoo clipped to my belt, I went wandering, discovering other satrapies and principalities.

The conclusion was not long in coming that the 34th Democratic National Convention, at this stage at least, was not for me. There were too many lines of authority looping back to the shadows. My forte in this game so far had been that of an independent producer working at a healthy remove from the seats of power. This was a good time to get lost. I put the buzzer on the "off" position so I would not hear any summons to the telephone and went walking. On a back street I bought a pair of crepe-soled shoes and proceeded to see Atlantic City.

I had been to Atlantic City once before, as a very young child on a family vacation, and retained three dim but distinct memories:

a white horse and its rider leaping from a platform into a tank of water; boardwalk chairs pushed by black men; green plants in a shining hotel lobby that opened on a sunny wooden walk. Now I was on that boardwalk once again. Were all the old planks gone, replaced? Many times, probably. A white horse and its rider were still jumping at the Steel Pier. The boardwalk chairs were motorized. The glisten had dulled.

A huge sign bearing Barry Goldwater's face and the slogan "In your heart, you know he's right" stretched across the roof of the Million Dollar Pier. I wonder who got hell for that. The old Jewish men and women from New York, mostly men, huddle in their stilled chairs on the boardwalk in the sun. The bodies on the beach. Game stalls. Auction houses. Chocolate candy. Ice cream. Taffy. Back off the beach. Cross Pacific Avenue. Pass through crowds of arriving conventioneers. Walk the parallel street. Atlantic Avenue. Who was it, Esteban, who walked parallel streets in *The Bridge of San Luis Rey*? Pawn shops with windows of things. Bars. One like a cool, brown tomb. Some cool, brown beers and shots of Scotch from a dark-green bottle. Night came by.

Wilson McCarthy arrived in town, and he and Underwood and I talked about our abnormal roles as advance men in a situation in which the crowds were built in, the program more or less out of our hands, and Bill Moyers present to call the shots directly. McCarthy said Underwood should handle the presidential box in the convention hall.

"You be in charge there, Marty. Take care of the guests. Run off the freeloaders."

I inherited the presidential birthday party, which was to follow the speeches accepting the presidential and vice presidential nominations. We split up again, and I began looking into the preparations for the birthday party. They were in an advanced stage. Somebody had ordered a mammoth cake with an outline of all the States of the Union on it. The style was unabashed corn. There was to be a sentimental recap of LBJ's humble beginnings by a master of ceremonies and then some sort of an ethnic charade featuring people in national costume. My contribution was a suggestion that made the party even cornier. There was a meeting on the party, and it turned out that although the script was written, the producers were waiting for a master of ceremonies to be selected.

"Name the Hollywood personality that you want," offered Lloyd Hand of California. "We'll get him."

Some names were mentioned.

"Hey," I said. "This is an ethnic extravaganza, isn't it? So how about the master ethnic, Danny Thomas?" Heads nodded.

"Done," said Hand. The meeting ended. Somewhere along the line, Thomas showed up, and there was a rehearsal, which he began to direct despite all the others who had their hand in the production. I sat down with him later and we talked about the show.

"We open with 'Danny Boy' and I come on," said Thomas.

I told him I did not think this an appropriate opening for the birthday party of a president who was not named "Danny." He joshed me, insisted, said that was the way it was done in show business. I did not care much about the opening music, but I had one demand: the sentimental introduction would have to be trimmed to about a minute. We got along amicably.

A network TV director asked me if I had any idea if the party could be filmed and if so where he could place the pool camera. I told him "sure" and indicated a place for the camera. He set up his camera gratefully, said he had been waiting several days for an answer.

There was a meeting with newspaper and TV people about the party. Suddenly I found myself being introduced as "The man who moves the president." Damn that phrase. McCarthy has been around. He loves those words to describe us.

The faces swung to me, and someone asked for the president's precise schedule on the day he accepts the nomination.

"Well, uh," I said. "We haven't decided just where we will, uh, move the president. I will let you know. Sometime."

Hour by hour Atlantic City was filling up. Someone told me that the Maine convention delegation was moving into a motel south on the boardwalk, so I went down to pay a visit. I told Senator Muskie and his staff what I knew about the convention schedule and then returned later for a cocktail party to which they invited me.

McCarthy had to look at a house down the beach that was being offered as a residence for the president when he stayed overnight on August 27. Several of us got into the limousine, which we had at our disposal by this time, and drove to the house. McCarthy went in with a Secret Service agent, but the rest of us stayed outside so there would not be a herd tracking sand through the place. Somebody, probably McCarthy, had told the chauffeur of the limousine that I was the governor of Colorado. He followed me around calling me "governor" and asking me questions about my state. I answered him with great invention.

He was still driving us when we staged the mock advance. Bill Moyers was flying to Atlantic City from Washington in a light plane with Douglass Cater, another member of the White House staff, as a second passenger. They were to land at night at Bader Field, the airport for small planes near the downtown area.

"Let's give them the treatment," said McCarthy.

We organized a motorcade of two cars, our limousine with the gullible driver and a shabby convertible. We had hand radios for communication. Underwood and I found fedoras made from gray cardboard in a novelty store. Wearing these grim hats, sunglasses, and gray suits, we could pass, at least at night, for Hollywood's version of Secret Service agents. Jerry Bruno, then nominally on the Democratic National Committee's staff but in the process of joining our unit, came along equipped with a toy plastic submachine gun.

When the light plane landed, Underwood and I went out on the apron and took the bags from the hands of the pilot. Moyers looked at us with great curiosity in the darkness, but we would not respond to his questions, and he could not figure out who was under the hats and behind the dark glasses. We ushered Moyers and Cater into the shabby convertible, and then we "security men" climbed into the comfortable limousine. Hal Pachios in the lead car opened radio contact with McCarthy, who was hidden in the recesses of the limousine.

A plainclothesman assigned to the airport to watch for shady characters coming into town had grown increasingly agitated at our behavior, despite the reassuring explanations we had made to him earlier. He had called for a superior who arrived as our motorcade was starting to roll. They both began to shout and to pound on the back of our limousine. The chauffeur was inclined to ignore them, since he had a governor and other important personages in the car. But we directed him to stop, and McCarthy rolled down a window. After a few minutes of fast talk, the motorcade was permitted to proceed, although the police officers were both shaking their heads. Down the highway we went, jargon flowing between the radios, Pachios pointing out real crossroads and nonexistent crowds. It was silly, but the regular advance was a bore. There was minor excitement later when it turned out that some security men not in on the gag had heard some of the radio chatter with alarm.

On the night of August 26, several of us were sitting around a room in the Pageant Motel, Johnson headquarters, next to the convention hall, when McCarthy put his head in and shouted "We've got a movement!" There was a spurt of activity as preparations were made to meet the president at the Atlantic City Airport and take him to the convention hall where he could recommend Senator Hubert Humphrey to the convention as his running mate. LBJ had wearied finally of the game of cat and mouse he had been playing at the White House over his vice presidential choice. He was not due at the convention until the following day to accept his own nomination, but apparently he could not resist extracting the last scrap of drama from the vice presidential selection. The recommendation was made and accepted, and Johnson returned to Washington.

August 27 was the climax of the convention. We hung around and did odd jobs. The presidential helicopter was to drop down on the parking lot near the convention hall, so we did some organizing in that area. Somebody came to me with a problem. The brightly dressed New Jersey Girls had been pushed back into the waiting crowd by police. Would I talk about this to Bill Duncan, who was in charge of security at Atlantic City for the Secret Service?

Duncan was standing in the parking lot speaking into a hand radio when I broached this important subject.

"John," he said, "I've got an alarm on a Puerto Rican who is supposed to be after the president and you give me this business about the New Jersey Girls."

I went back to my prompter and told him to take his problem about New Jersey Girls elsewhere.

The Puerto Rican scare proved to be a hoax.

Marvin Watson was uptight about this time at the angle of the television cameras positioned on the second-floor balcony of the hall. They pointed down at the signs and banners of civil rights activists protesting the lily-white Mississippi delegation.

"This is his big day," Watson said. "It's not right that they should be focusing on the protestors."

He suggested that we get the networks to move the cameras. We talked about it. By nightfall, the picketing was over and the signs were stacked. But another television difficulty arose in the shape of a tall cherry picker, a piece of construction equipment reared like a tyrannosaurus in front of the porch where the presidential party would stand to view the fireworks concluding the night's business. It was not the dinosaur-like machine that caused the trouble but its glaring eyes. The cherry picker carried a television camera and twin lights. I was standing on the porch when the TV crew tested the lights. They were blinding. I hunted up George Reedy, Johnson's press secretary, and pointed out the problem. He prevailed upon the television crew to cut off one of the lights, but even the remaining one was hard on the eyes.

I had been checking on final arrangements for the presidential birthday party and was not in the hall when long waves of applause held Robert Kennedy speechless at the podium and not there when the film made of the JFK years was shown. But I had an errand backstage and walked around the corridor and up the back stairs, my "all areas" pass clearing me through the checkpoints. I went past a security guard, who looked at me oddly, and came upon a weeping Bobby Kennedy sitting on a step in the stairwell, head in hands. I turned and went through the first door I could find.

Later when the speeches of acceptance were over the guests for the birthday party streamed to the upper room where the party was to start. A New Jersey state trooper posted at a side door stopped a knot of people and tried to send the group to a main entrance where they could be identified. One woman, a member of the White House staff, shouted in almost hysterical rage at being denied immediate admittance. Lloyd Hand came to the rescue and passed her through.

The crowd inside the room was so dense that movement was difficult. The president and his family entered and stepped up to the platform. Danny Thomas stood before LBJ and began his spiel. McCarthy and I helped Senator and Mrs. Humphrey up on the platform.

Thomas talked and talked and talked. He had every line of the prepared cornball speech and others of his own. I thought the president's smile became fixed. The costumed nationality bit followed, and then the president cut the cartographic cake and ate a slice of Texas. The party later won a well-earned booby award from the *Harvard Lampoon*.

When it came time to move to the porch to see the fireworks display on the beach, I linked hands with the Secret Service agents, and we moved the crowd back to extricate the principals. As we opened the way to the porch, Humphrey grabbed at me and said,

"Two of my children are missing. Can you find them and get them up here?"

I threaded my way downstairs and, with the help of some agents, found one of the two who had been swept downstairs in the wall-to-wall crowd. The second had to watch the fireworks from the boardwalk.

The fireworks roared and laced the sky, punctuating the nomination of Lyndon Baines Johnson for his own term as president of the United States and the selection of Hubert Horatio Humphrey as his running mate. From the upstairs porch, the nominees watched the squirts of color high above the beach and listened to the rising fusillades of explosives. Footmanlike, I and a few others stood behind them.

The next morning, August 28, 1964, President Johnson addressed the Democratic National Committee in a conference room of the convention hall and departed, triumphantly, for his ranch in Texas.

I went for a long walk on the beach.

CHAPTER 4

The Road to Reassurance

The state of the craft of political poll taking being what it was by 1964, both Lyndon Baines Johnson and Barry Goldwater must have been aware by the start of September that Johnson would be elected in November unless there was some cataclysmic political upheaval. But Lyndon Johnson had been called, facetiously, "Landslide Johnson" in 1948, when he was elected to the United States Senate by an 87-vote margin in a statewide Texas race. His reelections had been much more respectable, and yet one suspects that reassurances were still needed, especially since it is unlikely that he ever would have become president if the office had not devolved upon him. He provided his own reassurances. Between his nomination on August 27 in Atlantic City and his election on November 2, he traveled 50,050 statute miles by plane—twice the distance around the earth. And this does not take into account the local traveling he did when he got where he was going by airplane.

There was no respite after the convention. The Democratic campaign was to begin on Labor Day, September 7, in the stronghold of the workingman, Detroit. President Johnson would speak in Cadillac Square just before noon. I was dispatched with an advance crew to prepare the way. One of my helpers had a penchant for office space and immediately obtained an office and secretarial help in the Democratic State Central Committee headquarters. We heard from him occasionally thereafter. Another assistant, a youngster on his first advance, proved more helpful. He made contact with Democratic youth groups who turned out signs of welcome and were generally useful.

Wilson McCarthy sent Jerry Bruno after us as a crowd builder. I did not care for split responsibilities. I also knew that Bruno was an old hand at advancing Detroit for John Kennedy. It was a city in which I had never been before. So I called Bruno aside after hearing him on the telephone with McCarthy and said "You've advanced this place, Jerry. You know how to make it go. Suppose we fix it up so you run this advance?"

"No, no," he said. "I'll just work on the crowds. I won't get into the program or anything like that."

The schedule called for the president to fly to the Metropolitan Airport and then helicopter to Civic Center Park on the riverfront where Cobo Hall is situated. The president would greet retired members of the United Auto Workers (UAW) union who were meeting at the hall and then motorcade to the Sheraton-Cadillac Hotel and wait for the cue to descend on Cadillac Square as the preliminary speaking program ended.

One of my first calls was on Detroit's young Mayor, Jerome Cavanagh, at City Hall. We talked generally about arrangements, and he was cooperative. But when I came to the part about helicopters landing in the civic center parking area, he grinned.

"You're sure you're giving it to me straight?"

"What d'you mean?"

"I'm thinking of what happened here before. I had to have the light poles taken down so the helicopters could land. Two thousand dollars. What happened? They came in by motorcade. No helicopters."

"This is the way it's supposed to be, mayor, but let me pin it down so there's no mistake."

I received assurances from Washington later and passed them on to the mayor.

"You're sure?"

"Positive."

"Okay."

Shortly before Labor Day, Republicans were criticizing the use of presidential aircraft on political trips. On September 5, Johnson told a press conference that the Democratic Party would pay the expenses of the trip to Detroit. The use of helicopters at Detroit was scrubbed. When I got the word, I called Mayor Cavanagh.

"Mayor, you know the plans to helicopter the president into that area by Cobo Hall?"

"I know them very, very well."

He also knew, as did I, that the crews that take down light poles had done their work.

"Yeah."

"You bum."

"Righto."

I met several times with Al Barbour, president of the Wayne County AFL-CIO, which was sponsoring the Labor Day rally. I also had lunch with former Michigan Governor John B. Swainson, who provided helpful political advice. I made him head of the reception committee for the president. Then, with Bruno, I went to see the man at the heart of Detroit's unionism, Walter Reuther, "the redhead," president of the United Auto Workers Union.

We had to wait in an anteroom at Solidarity House, the union's headquarters. The UAW was in the midst of negotiations with Chrysler, and a strike appeared to be a possibility at that point, although it did not materialize.

Joseph Rauh, the Washington lawyer, came out of Reuther's office, and we went in.

"We're advance men," I said.

Reuther smiled. "So I gathered. I've been expecting you. What can we do?"

Bruno and I shook hands with him. I tried to give him a hearty handshake, forgetting about the shotgun blast that had injured his arm. We settled for touching fingers.

I said that the program looked fine, but that the crowds in that big square might be a problem. We had been told that it was not easy to get out the union families anymore on a holiday when the parks and beaches beckoned.

Reuther said, "We can help on this."

Pat Greathouse, UAW vice president, was assigned to work on crowds. Bruno and Pat Kennedy had teamed up with him. Our advance team was impressed with the United Auto Workers operation. Pat Kennedy said later that the UAW operatives were "politically sophisticated and extremely well organized." The turnout for the rally was excellent. The union arranged for free parking in the Cadillac Square area and chartered buses to take workers and their families and friends living in outlying areas to and from the downtown square.

The Democratic State Central Committee worked up some costumed ethnic demonstrations for the motorcade route between Cobo Hall and the Sheraton-Cadillac. We did some crowd building for the airport. Ronald Pontius, the Secret Service agent in charge of security, became irritated when Bruno criticized his choice of a downtown exit from the airport expressway. Bruno claimed it would be impossible to build a crowd along the exit road, which was partly an underpass. I was indifferent, because the crowd would start in the vicinity of Cobo Hall. But since the issue was raised, we had to resolve it. After some hard feelings were aroused, the exit was changed so that the motorcade would leave the expressway closer to the crowd.

Labor Day was a hot one. There was a fair crowd at the airport, but we were not worried about the greeting there. Cadillac Square was our concern, and we had concentrated our efforts on turning out people there. Stepping lively in a futile effort to keep out of the range of the clicking camera of a White House photographer, I introduced the president to the reception committee when he came down from his plane. There were scattered groups along the freeway and a good crowd in the Cobo Hall area. Newspapers, not the major Detroit papers that were out on strike, estimated the crowd at Cadillac Square at 100,000. Let's say there were a lot of people.

When the motorcade reached the hotel and the presidential party went to the prepared reception rooms, I moved to Cadillac Square and kept in touch with the hotel by telephone from the platform. Or, rather, the hotel kept in touch with me. The president was tired of waiting for the other orators to stop talking. Finally, I receive an ultimatum: "Ready or not, here we come." Congressman Neil Staebler, the Democratic candidate for governor, was at the microphone. I stepped to the podium and put a note in large letters before him: "THE PRESIDENT IS ON HIS WAY." The hotel was just down the street.

Staebler continued for a few more minutes. Governor George Romney, his opponent, had spoken previously and had been lightly heckled by the partisan crowd. The Republican governor had been invited to participate, even though Labor Day exercises in Cadillac Square had become Democratic rallies. It had been recalled that a year earlier he had shown up in the crowd, uninvited, in shirt sleeves and eating popcorn, to the delight of news photographers.

While Staebler was winding down, I was leading other Democratic politicians one by one from the back of the platform, placing them in position to greet the president in range of the photographers' lenses. By the time I escorted Staebler to the rear, Governor Romney was looking lonely.

The platform from which Johnson spoke was in John F. Kennedy Plaza, close to the spot where Kennedy had opened his campaign four years earlier. The crowd stretched far back into the recesses of Cadillac Square. His words were not harshly partisan but were an appeal for broadly based support. It was consensus politics, a brand that was to become familiar in the months ahead.

There was one swipe at the bomb rattling of his Republican opponent, Barry Goldwater.

"Make no mistake," said Johnson. "There is no such thing as a conventional nuclear weapon." But his address opening the campaign was hardly a ripsnorter:

". . . So today I have come here in Cadillac Square to call for national unity. . . . Responsible business knows that fair wages are essential to its prosperity. Responsible labor knows that fair profits are essential to rising employment. Farmers and city dwellers, bankers and laborers know that by strengthening each group we strengthen the Nation—by pursuing the growth of all, we advance the welfare of each."

Even in the heartland of labor on Labor Day he was picking his way down the middle of the road. His flamboyance was restricted to his manner of greeting the crowd, waving his broad hat, darting from his escorts into clumps of people, and clutching hands. One of his own hands was bloodied on this day in the fury of hand clasping. And he nearly lost his Texas hat. A determined souvenir hunter grabbed the waving brim, but the big Johnson fist held on. Then it was over. The cars headed for the airport. The plane took off. I experienced what had become a familiar sensation, a feeling of lightheadedness, relief. Air Force One was in the air, heading elsewhere.

Back in Washington, following the Detroit trip, I settled into a spell of manning the desk in our advance office at the Democratic National Committee on K Street. The office doors bore signs suggested by Atlantic City: "In your heart, you know it's shut." The motive in posting them probably was partly arrogant, but they did dissuade other staff members of the committee from making the room a gathering place. Considering President Johnson's mania for secrecy, it would have been imprudent to have many ears present in a room in which information about his future movements was being bandied about.

A pool of advance men had been formed while I was in Detroit, and I added a few names myself. The typed list of advance men that we were using by mid-campaign had forty-five names, but only about half that number were regulars. In the latter part of the campaign less than a dozen men bore the brunt of the trips, having proved themselves in action. Besides the names on the list, however, there were numerous other men who were pressed into service for one reason or another for individual stops. There were three secretaries at first, Peggy Stark, Sherrie Huberman, and Sammie Bear, later joined by Freddie Brawley, daughter of southern campaign coordinator Bill Brawley. Sherrie was a tall, freckle-faced redhead who had worked in Marvin Watson's office at the Democratic National Convention and who remembered me as the man who never answered his radio buzzer in Atlantic City. Peggy was the heart of the operation. She moved the paperwork and kept in touch with Wilson McCarthy, if anyone could be said to have been in touch with him. A pleasant, angular girl, she tried to get McCarthy to answer his telephone calls. Wilson McCarthy—I was in his company regularly in those days, but I did not know him well. About six feet tall, thirty-three years old, darkly handsome, dressed with style, he brightened the eyes of many a female. McCarthy had a small house in Georgetown, so narrow you almost had to enter it sideways. I was there a few times when we brought in orders of spareribs after late working sessions. The Secret Service insisted that he have a home telephone while he was chief advance man for the president. He had occasion to use the telephone one night while I was there, taking it from a drawer where it lay unplugged, wrapped in a towel.

A couple of times he told me, "I've learned to look out for myself. Nobody else will." When there was doubt of his whereabouts, Alper and Meyers Custom Tailors in Baltimore was a good place to check. Herbie Alper, rotund and politically hep, was his tailor. Stylists were impressed by the fact that McCarthy designed his own shoes and had them custom made. Wilson McCarthy—there was a trace of Edwin Arlington Robinson's "Flammonde."

Also crowded into that advance boiler room in the Democratic headquarters were Marty Underwood, Harold Pachios, Jerry Bruno, and Dick O'Hare. Underwood, my like number as McCarthy's other deputy, was older than most of us. He came from the Midwest, where he had worked for the Schaeffer Pen Company in Iowa and had done some work for Mayor Richard Daley in Chicago before becoming a Kennedy advance man and later an employee of the U.S. Department of Commerce. Pachios, of Greek descent, from Portland, Maine, had been in the Peace Corps headquarters with McCarthy and was a sporadic law student at Georgetown University. O'Hare, a towering gray-haired lawyer, was Kenny O'Donnell's representative in the campaign. The most knowledgeable man in the room about political scheduling, O'Hare was barely used. His Kennedy ties had been too strong. He came in to the office almost daily and doggedly sat out the days.

Bruno formally joined the presidential advance group. Earlier he had been assigned other duties by National Committee Chairman John Bailey. Bruno was best known as the advance man for John and Robert Kennedy's campaigns. Another Italian American who was on the Democratic National Committee staff, Mel Cottone sat in a nearby office and worked closely with our unit. Volunteer George Lusk did the same. The full resources of the committee, of course, were available.

In retrospect, it is surprising that the unit was able to maintain such a low profile. Except for Drew Pearson's post-election column and the occasional stories when advance men were put on the spot by reporters in the field, there was little or no journalistic mention of this group that served as the cutting edge of the 1964 Johnson campaign. Even afterward it was ignored. Theodore H. White, in his *The Making of the President 1964*, describes a variety of LBJ election "teams" but manages to get through his book without mentioning the unit that leveled the way for Johnson. Columnists Rowland Evans and Robert Novak, in their book *Lyndon B. Johnson: The Exercise of Power*, went so far as to make the claim that because of President Johnson's idiosyncratic response to orderly scheduling, advance men "became superfluous" in the campaign. Here is delayed news: Advance teams were out in front of President Johnson everywhere he campaigned during the two months before the 1964 elections. And besides, some sat around at a few locations where, for one reason or another, he decided not to go after the forerunners had been dispatched.

The deskman for the advance unit had no difficulty keeping busy when word came from the White House as to where the president wanted to go, and when. Although these instructions often included specific events in which the president definitely was to participate, many times it was up to us to "create" suitable events. Advance men had to be selected, briefed, ticketed, and sent on their way, and the deskman had to keep in touch with them from then on. Arrangements made in the field had to be checked and approved every step of the way. New instructions had to be given to the advance men on the scene. Appeals to the advance desk from local politicos had to be listened to courteously. Touchy problems had to be discussed with Johnson's closest assistants. Working hours many times stretched beyond midnight. With McCarthy making survey sweeps in front of the president and Underwood out on advance trips, I was almost constantly on the desk in the weeks immediately after Detroit.

Johnson went to Harrisburg, Pennsylvania, on September 10. On the 11th, he was in Jacksonville, Florida, and Brunswick, Georgia, to check on the effects of Hurricane Dorn, a natural event that we had not arranged. On September 15, he spoke in Miami Beach and received a briefing at Cape Kennedy. His first sustained trip was to the Northwest, September 16–18: Great Falls, Montana; Vancouver, British Columbia (reaching a bit); Seattle, Washington; Portland, Oregon; Sacramento, California; Salt Lake City, Utah. On September 20, he was in Morgantown, West Virginia, and on September 22 in Atlantic City again, this time speaking to the convention of the United Steelworkers of America. There was a major trip to the Southwest, September 25–27. Johnson met President Lopez Mateos of Mexico in El Paso, Texas, to mark the settling of an old boundary dispute, and then, in rapid succession, he visited Muskogee, Eufala Dam, and Oklahoma City, Oklahoma, and Texarkana, Texas, before heading for the LBJ Ranch. The pace was stepping up.

Advance men's manuals were floating around the headquarters of the Democratic National Committee in the 1964 campaign, but we settled for a simple checklist developed by several of us, which was handed out to advance men as they were sent on their way. It indicates the amount of detail for which a Johnson advance man was responsible:

Checklist for Advance Men on Presidential Visits

(The following list of questions is provided as a guide to some of the more important elements that you, as an advance man, should thoroughly check out as part of your preparation for a presidential visit to any area. This list is not meant to be exhaustive—there are many area problems or special problems that you should take into consideration for the specific project in which you are engaged.)

I. Party Organization

Have you made contact and enlisted the support of:

1. The local party office?
2. The party's state coordinator?
3. The local Women's activities chairman?
4. The J464 (Johnson for '64) group?
5. The local area Citizens for Johnson chairman?
6. The head of the Johnson girls in the area?
7. The local nationalities groups?
8. The Senior Citizens group?
9. The Republicans for Johnson?
10. The Independents for Johnson?
11. The Young Citizens for Johnson?

II. Public Officials

Have you enlisted the support, where practical, of:

1. The governor?
2. The mayor?
3. The county officials in the area?
4. The superintendent of schools (in order to have the schoolchildren released and bands provided?)

III. Business, Union, and Civic Organizations

Have you enlisted the support, where possible, of the following organizations:

1. The Chamber of Commerce?
2. The Board of Trade?
3. The Downtown Merchants Association?
4. Service Clubs?
5. Veterans organizations?
6. Unions?

IV. The Route

1. Have you examined the route thoroughly for maximum crowd participation?
2. Have you seen to it that materials have been distributed along the route for placement?
3. Have you seen to it that crowds have been assured at important intersections and squares?

V. Signs

1. Have you made special assignments for the production of signs, both printed and handmade, and have you checked that such signs are actually being produced and will be ready and available?
2. Have you made provisions for the posting of large signs on important buildings?

VI. Crowds and Bands

1. Have you concentrated crowds along the most important parts of the route?
2. How many bands have been obtained, and have you placed them with full consideration given to helping build crowds?

VII. Materials

1. Have you checked the local Democratic Central Committee to see if they have ordered campaign materials from the National Committee; if they have received them; and if they will make good use of them on the date of the president's appearance?
2. Have you taken an advance man's campaign materials kit with you? [This included pins and other geegaws as well as big round stickers which I had designed bearing an arrow and "LBJ Route." They were to be attached in the dark of the night to telephone poles along the motorcade route.]

VIII. Speaking Site

1. Have you examined personally the area of the speaking site, giving maximum consideration to allowing the crowd close proximity to the president, consistent with security requirements?

2. Have you personally checked out the sound system—a meeting should be set up with the owner of the sound equipment two days prior to the president's arrival: the sound should be ready to test a day before the president arrives.

3. Are you assured that a proper lectern has been obtained?

4. Have you checked the press area?

IX. Transportation

1. Have you made sure that transportation has been provided for the White House press, and that the local press needs have been taken care of?

2. Have you made sure that at least one station wagon has been obtained for rapid transportation of White House communications equipment?

3. Are the buses that have been obtained for either press or VIP guests use sufficiently powerful (Greyhound type) to keep up with a motorcade?

X. Miscellaneous

1. Have you provided the central advance office with full information about the proposed program; the names of important party and other personages whom the president might be expected to mention?

2. Have you investigated how many radio and TV stations will carry the program live, and how many other stations plan to provide lesser type coverage?

3. Have you personally checked out the number, kind, and seating capacity of the automobiles being used in the motorcade?

4. Have you worked out a proposed list of personages to be seated in the motorcade?

5. Have you made sure that fire extinguishers are available in the cars near the front and rear of the motorcade?

6. Have you furnished the central advance office with any proposed ancillary functions to the main program (i.e. club meetings, greetings by the president to particular persons, etc.)?

7. Have you established good working relationships with the daily and weekly newspapers in the area, as well as radio and TV stations?

8. Has the route been amply publicized?

9. Have you obtained from the local area an ample supply of bull-horns for the president's arrival?

10. Have as many local Johnson girls as possible been provided? [These were colorfully dressed girls to serve as hostesses for the various functions.]

The extensive instructions were more hortatory than realistic.

The copy of our checklist, which I found in my grocery carton archives, is undated, but the reminder about fire extinguishers in motorcades is internal evidence that this version dates after the New England trip, September 28–29, because it was then that fire extin-guishers suddenly became a matter of concern. The engine of one of the cars in the motorcade had caught fire in Providence, Rhode Island. The item about bullhorns supports the post-New England dating, because it was on that trip that LBJ became bullhorn happy. Any clump of spectators could become the object of the president's impromptu oratory, and he could use the horns to bellow personal invitations to curbside crowds to "Come to the speakin'."

The checklist sometimes was helpful. But the advance team on the scene was expected to concentrate on the most important ele-ments that would contribute to the success of the stop for which it was responsible, elements on or off the list, often off. For instance, although problems with individual congressmen whose districts were to be visited were supposed to be handled on the Washington end, they often were not solved there. An alert advance man who could deal cooperatively but firmly with congressional figures and their staffs proved invaluable to our operation. A harbinger long on his own importance as a representative of the president and short on an appreciation of a congressman's problems in his own district could raise havoc.

The days went by on K Street, and the hours grew long. Advance crews were calling in from around the country night and day to obtain approval of arrangements made locally and to request, sometimes to plead for, information about the president's schedule that would affect their stop. Sometimes the deskman could help, but LBJ's wall of secrecy was hard to pierce, even by those hired to, and trying to, serve him. We were not the only ones hampered by the president's love of secrecy. Speechwriters such as Secretary of Labor Willard Wirtz frequently were on the telephone seeking better information than they possessed about the president's schedule. Sometimes we were barely able to get advance men in place and operating before the president's arrival, but usually we had enough time to do an adequate job. In the room on K Street, advance teams of two, three, or more men were being assembled, briefed, and dispatched continually. Others, between trips, were coming through for approval of their expense vouchers. Jack Valenti or another White House assistant would be on the line demanding to know where Wilson McCarthy could be reached. Days in the room where telephones were always ringing and where doors, despite what you might know in your heart, were always opening, went on, and on.

CHAPTER 5

New England's Wild Endorsement

I finally broke away from K Street when President Johnson went to New England. You know, even at this late date I am not sure how Johnson's campaign schedule was worked out. Some political writers credited Kenneth O'Donnell with masterminding the schedule, but it was clear to me that his role was slight. O'Donnell, a shrewd political operator, was also a Kennedy man. Johnson was not relying heavily on Kennedy men for advice on where he should campaign. Dick O'Hare would prepare a schedule for O'Donnell, and that would be the end of it. O'Donnell did sit in on meetings where schedules were discussed and roughed out, however. He came into our quarters now and again, mostly to see O'Hare. Both told me that they really had no role in scheduling.

When I was on the desk, it did not matter to me who was making the decisions. All I wanted was to know them early enough in time to get our people out in front of the president in time to do some good. Most often the word came from Wilson McCarthy, but sometimes directly from Moyers or Valenti, and later Marvin Watson. I was working the desk when we were notified of the New England campaign schedule: six stops in one day, September 28. Johnson was planning to blitz New England. I began to round up advance men and, as more information was given to me, to put together a schedule. I wrote an original version and three revisions in all, and am looking at a copy of the final version as I write this. It was the schedule we had in hand on that tumultuous day, September 28, spilling over to September 29, when President Johnson saw hundreds of thousands of people face-to-face. The script was not followed exactly. Times got out of whack because of the crowds. And there were other changes, such as the arrival of senators and congressmen on the presidential aircraft rather than their scheduled presence on the ground to welcome the president at the airports in their home states. But the New England schedule is a good example of how the bare bones of a decision to campaign in certain localities in 1964 were fleshed out:

September 27, 1964 Revision #3
NEW ENGLAND SCHEDULE
September 28, 1964

7:55 a.m.	Leave White House
8:00	Leave National Airport
9:30	Arrive Theodore Green Airport, Providence, Rhode Island

Senator Pastore will board the aircraft and escort the president down the ramp. The reception committee will consist of the following persons:
Senator Pell
Congressman Fogarty
Congressman St. Germain
Governor Chafee
Barnaby Keeney, President Brown University
Mrs. Keeney
Liz Keeney (11-year-old daughter of Brown's president)
Lt. Gov. Gallogly
Mayor Hobbs of Warwick (since the airport is physically in the town of Warwick)

The president will also stop to shake hands with the newly appointed chairman of the Citizens for Johnson for Rhode Island, Mr. Arthur Damord. Pictures will be taken with Mr. Damord and Lt. Gov. Gallogly

The president will then walk over to a car in which former Senator Green will

	be seated, enter car and talk with the senator. Then motorcade begins (The senator will return to his home)
9:40	The president will depart in the motorcade, riding with President Keeney, Senators Pastore and Pell
	The second car will have Mrs. Johnson, Mrs. Keeney, and Liz Keeney
	The third VIP car will have Congressman Fogarty, Congressman St. Germain, and Governor Chafee
10:02	Arrive Meehan Auditorium, Brown University and enter trailer where Howard Curtis, secretary of the university, assists President Johnson into a cap and gown
10:07	President is escorted into auditorium by President Keeney, H. S. McLeod (vice chancellor of the university), Governor Chafee and mace bearer
10:10	President arrives platform and is seated with President Keeney, McLeod, Pusey (president of Harvard), John Nicholas Brown, of the board of fellows of Brown, and Brown University Chaplain Baldwin
10:11	National Anthem
10:13	Invocation by Chaplain Baldwin
10:15	Greetings by President Keeney
10:20	Greetings by Governor Chafee
10:25	Greetings from President Pusey on behalf of all N.E. colleges
10:30	President begins speech (live TV)
10:50	President concludes speech and leaves platform

10:55	President's car departs for airport
11:20	President arrives airport
11:25	President departs Providence for Hartford
11:50	President arrives Rentschler Airport and is greeted by the following persons:

Governor and Mrs. Dempsey
Senator Ribicoff
Senator Dodd
Congressman Emilio Daddario
William Gwinn, president, United
  Aircraft Corp.
John M.Bailey
Other members of the Connecticut
  Congressional Delegation

President enters limousine with Dempsey, Ribicoff, Dodd and Daddario

Mrs. Johnson is in the second limousine with Mrs. Dempsey, Mrs. Dodd, Mrs. Daddario, and Mrs. Bailey—Mrs. Ribicoff is not expected

11:55	Motorcade departs for Hartford, starting down Willow Street—United Aircraft workers line street
12:10 p.m.	Motorcade arrives Hartford TIMES Building, side entrance

President is met by Publisher, Kenneth Burke, and they proceed to Mr. Burke's office

Dignitaries and White House Press proceed to portico

12:11	President arrives at Mr. Burke's office
12:16	President is accompanied by Mr. Burke to portico
12:18	John Bailey introduces Governor Dempsey

12:19	Governor Dempsey introduces Senator Dodd
12:20	Senator Dodd introduces president
12:21	President speaks
12:41	President concludes speech
12:51	President enters limousine and departs for Constitution Plaza
12:54	President arrives State Street entrance of Constitution Plaza and is met by Arthur Lumsden (executive director of the Greater Hartford Chamber of Commerce), and J. Doyle DeWitt (president, Travelers Insurance Company)
	Mr. Lumsden escorts the president up to meet assembled key corporation and newspaper executives
1:15	President leaves Constitution Plaza reception and motorcade departs for Rentschler Field
1:45	President departs Hartford for Burlington
3:00	Arrive Burlington, Vermont Municipal Airport President is greeted by: Phil Hoff, Governor Frederick Fayette, Democratic candidate for senator Bernard O'Shea, Democratic candidate for Congress Other local dignitaries
3:15	President speaks
3:35	President completes speaking
3:50	President departs for Portland, Maine

4:50	President arrives Portland Municipal Airport and is greeted by:
	Senator and Mrs. Edmund Muskie
	William D. Hathaway (Democratic candidate for Congress, 2nd District and also chairman of the Democratic State Committee)
	Kenneth Curtis (Democratic candidate for Congress, 1st District)
	Governor John Reed (Republican)
	Richard Dubord, national committeeman
	Mrs. Fay Broderick, national committeewoman
	Miss Judith Mackenson, vice chairman of Maine State Democratic Committee
4:55	Motorcade departs airport
	President will ride with Senator Muskie and candidates Curtis and Hathaway. Mrs. Johnson will ride separately with Mrs. Muskie
5:15	President arrives City Hall Plaza and proceeds to platform with Senator Muskie and two candidates
5:18	President is welcomed to Portland by Honorable J. Weston Walch, chairman, Portland City Council (Republican)
5:19	Brief remarks of welcome by Senator Muskie and introduction of the president
5:24	President speaks
5.44	President leaves platform accompanied by Senator Muskie and Messrs. Curtis and Hathaway
5:50	Motorcade departs City Hall

6:05	Arrive airport
6.10	Depart Portland
6:45	Arrive Manchester, New Hampshire airport
6:55	Leave Manchester Airport by motorcade
7.15	Arrive Carpenter Motor Inn, President goes directly to private room
7:50	Dedication of office of Democratic Headquarters
7:55	President goes to grand ballroom
8:00	President addresses the Weekly Newspaper Editors Association of New Hampshire (live TV)
	There will be approximately 350 guests, which is total capacity
8:30	President leaves grand ballroom
8:35	President leaves Carpenter Motor Inn
8.55	President arrives Manchester Airport
9:00	President leaves Manchester
9:25	Arrives Logan International Airport in Boston
9:45	Arrives New England Baptist Hospital for visit

The first step, long before that final schedule was written, was to get advance teams out to the various locations. I called on Dick Walsh, a longtime Washington lawyer and a graduate of Brown University, to head the advance team at Providence. Two young executive types, Padraic Kennedy and Tom Kelley, were sent to Hartford, where part of the program would be devoted to wooing big businessmen. Chuck Lipsen, a brash labor union official, was sent to Burlington, where the visit was to consist of an airport speech and a handshaking rodeo.

Hal Pachios, a native of Maine, was to go to Portland to head the advance effort there. Wilson McCarthy suggested that I contact Warren O'Donnell, a Worcester, Massachusetts, businessman, who was Kenny O'Donnell's younger brother, to handle the Manchester advance. I did not know Warren at that time, but I called him up and he agreed to go. Other advance men were assembled to assist, and the teams were dispatched. When they reached their destinations and began operating, the telephone dialogs began about the programs and crowd-building activities in each city to be visited.

Well before the day for the president's tour, McCarthy and I, Assistant White House Press Secretary Malcolm Kilduff, some Secret Service agents, and a few others flew around the route, inspecting the sites with the advance men already on the scene. Some of us had a few Bloody Marys as we traveled. Mac Kilduff, who admitted to some partying the night before, fell asleep before Burlington and snored through that stop. The rest of us walked around the Burlington airport with Lipsen and decided on the place where the president would speak. We told Lipsen to arrange for a stand-up microphone, which meant no lectern. Later in the trip, Kilduff smote his head. "Hey! We forgot Burlington!" He was reassured.

In the annals of presidential campaign trips, September 28–29, 1964, must be in a class by itself for the sheer stamina of the candidate and the huge and boisterous crowds. Setting out from Washington's National Airport about 8 a.m. in the morning of September 28, Johnson visited all six New England states. He finally returned to the White House, buffeted, hands clawed, and, I imagine, supremely delighted, shortly before 4:30 a.m. the next day, September 29. I had never before seen such enthusiastic crowds. In Providence they were so wild they were fearsome.

I rode a press plane in front of the president on the trip and a rear car in the motorcades. Problems were not long in developing. When the press plane set down at the airport in the outskirts of Providence, I found Dick Walsh embroiled in an argument, one that was of our making in Washington. Walsh was under instructions from us to arrange the motorcade so that Rhode Island Senators John O. Pastore and Claiborne Pell and Brown President Barnaby C. Keeney would ride with President Johnson in the first car behind the leading police car. Republican Governor John H. Chafee was to be relegated to the third car, where he was to ride with Democratic Congressmen

John E. Fogarty and Fernand J. St. Germain. We were not promoting Republican officeholders on this trip.

Keeney, Chafee, Walsh, and a couple of others were gathered in a knot when I arrived. Chafee obviously was angry. Walsh turned and introduced me to the others, quickly summarizing the disagreement.

"I never heard of such a thing," said the governor, "a president coming into a state and slighting the host, the governor."

"Well you see, governor," I said, "when there are United States senators involved, protocol calls for them to ride with the president rather than the governor riding with him. That's the way we do it all the time. No offense to you. There aren't enough seats."

"That's not protocol as I understand it," said Chafee. Keeney was shaking his high-domed head. He said something about the relationship between the university and the state of Rhode Island and added, "You fellows have put me in a fine spot."

Keeney looked up at the presidential plane coming in for a landing. He began to walk away.

"I'll catch a taxicab," he said over his shoulder. "See you at the university."

I stopped him.

"Hold on," I said. "I'll work it out as soon as Number One is on the ground."

The presidential plane rolled to a stop, and president and Mrs. Johnson came down, followed by the entourage. They moved through the reception line. Wilson McCarthy had been riding in the presidential plane, and I pulled him aside as he came down the stairs. I laid out the problem to Senator Pell, who also had descended from the plane and was standing to one side. We asked him if he would ride in one of the cars behind the president. "I'll do anything that the president wants," Pell said, moving toward the reception line. It seemed to us that he was implying that the president rather than minions should ask him.

"Damn," I said. "Let's try Senator Pastore." Pastore took in the problem quickly and grinned. "I'll take care of it," he said. "Relax."

Pastore was up for reelection, but Pell was not. He walked over to Pell, and they exchanged a few words. Later, when the motorcade was ready to move, Governor Chafee had Pell's seat in the presidential car, and Pell rode in one of the following automobiles. Keeney did not take a taxicab.

When he was through the reception line, Johnson went over to a parked limousine, where the old and frail former Senator Theodore Green awaited him. They talked. Then the president took to the fences, and the New England trip was off to its tumultuous start. A fence was knocked flat as a crowd swarmed over it. President Johnson grabbed hands. There was a special irony to the hours that followed as Lyndon Johnson, president of the United States, rode through New England streets so packed that his car was brought to a halt, plunged into screaming groups of people, bloodied his hands, put himself into barely controllable situations. The President's Commission on the Assassination of President Kennedy, the Warren Commission, had issued its report the day before. The commission found that Lee Harvey Oswald alone was responsible for the death of President Kennedy. But its conclusions and recommendations focused on shortcomings in the methods used to protect presidents and called for improvements. One conclusion, number 12, was in the forefront of the minds of some on that New England trip:

> The commission recognizes that the varied responsibilities of the president require that he make frequent trips to all parts of the United States and abroad. Consistent with their high responsibilities presidents can never be protected from every potential threat. The Secret Service's difficulty in meeting its protective responsibility varies with the activities and the nature of the occupant of the Office of President and his willingness to conform to plans for his safety. In appraising the performance of the Secret Service it should be understood that it has to work within such limitations. Nevertheless, the commission believes that recommendations for improvements in presidential protection are compelled by the facts disclosed in this investigation.

The occupant of the Office of the President on this day climbed from his convertible in Rhode Island and walked nearly a mile along Occupasstuxet Road and the Post Road, handshaking and talking his way toward Brown University. The scheduled time for the trip from the airport to the university, checked out by our advance team, was twenty-two minutes. It took President Johnson's motorcade nearly one and a half hours. Crowds were thick everywhere, and Kennedy Plaza and LaSalle Square in Providence were roadblocks of people.

Some young girls screamed as though they were taking part in those marvelous events at Salem, Massachusetts, in 1692. The jacket of Secret Service agent John Chipps was ripped down the back and his trousers along the seams. A friendly photographer provided some tape to hold his trousers together.

The creeping pace on a sunny day was too much for a new Lincoln convertible in the motorcade borrowed for the occasion and driven by Detective Donald Kennedy of the Providence Police Department. The engine went afire, and flames shot from under the hood. The passengers, Admiral George C. Burkley, who was the president's physician, Jack Valenti, and Secret Service agents, jumped out. Up ahead the president's car spurted forward as the Secret Service passed the word about the fire. When it was determined that the trouble was just an automotive malfunction, the old speed was resumed.

Finally, the motorcade pulled up to Meehan Auditorium at the university, where the president entered a trailer parked near the doors and, inside, donned academic robes and a decorous expression before joining the convocation procession. Addresses tire me, so I wandered out of the auditorium, returning to the trailer to talk with Sergeant Paul Glynn, who was serving as the president's batman. I treated myself to one of the 7-Ups that had been provided for the president's dressing room. When the president reentered the trailer, he received a brisk toweling from Glynn and a fresh shirt. The time schedule was awry, so we hurried to the cars. The president rode to the airport in a closed limousine. But before boarding his plane he shook the hand of every member of the police detail within reach.

Hartford was a repeat of Providence, but the airport was closer. The crowds continued to be astonishingly thick. When the motorcade bogged down a few blocks from *The Hartford Times*, I got out of the vehicle in which I was riding and walked over to the *Times* where the president was to speak from the portico. Arrangements were shipshape. When the president arrived and began to speak, he paid the usual hyperbolic tribute to his political allies, which never failed to amuse me:

> Governor Dempsey; my longtime friend and valued adviser, Tom Dodd; your able and courageous Senator Abe Ribicoff; Congressman Daddario; all members of the most effective Connecticut delegation to the Congress; my old and trusted and helpful friend who may get us elected, John Bailey; your distinguished Mayor Glynn; my fellow Americans:

He Mark Antonied the crowd: "I don't intend to and I guess it is not necessary to talk politics . . ." And then he talked politics. The response was enthusiastic, so he played further upon the crowd: "Are we going to be united in November?" The answering roar was affirmative.

We proceeded to Constitution Plaza, which was close by, and there LBJ put his brand on the Hartford fat cats, also personally inviting other onlookers to bypass the ropes and "gather 'round." One bewildered policeman received a loud bawling out from the commander in chief for not letting the public through the ropes. Johnson gave the businessmen a Sam Rayburn story, which they laughed at, and they gave him a Charter Oak Leadership Medal, for which he thanked them. So that was Hartford.

There was hell to pay at the Burlington airport. When Jack Valenti, LBJ's short shadow, came out of the plane, he looked at the stand-up microphone and said "Where's the lectern?"

We told him that there wasn't one, that we had understood the president was to give one of his off-the-cuff airport speeches.

"He has a speech," said Valenti. "At all these stops you have to have lecterns."

Chuck Lipsen, McCarthy, and I raced for the terminal building, while the president went to the fences where, Vermont Democrats were later to claim, "the biggest crowd at any political gathering in Vermont's history" was cheering. With directions from the airport manager, we clattered into the basement and found an old lectern that could be built up to the right height with the Coca Cola boxes that were stacked in the lobby. In the meantime, the communications team had come up with another lectern. Johnson had two places to lay his speech when he finished shaking hands with members of the crowd. In the background, McCarthy was giving Lipsen hell.

"Hey," I said, "why holler at him? We told him to put up a stand-up mike?"

McCarthy thought for a moment. "You know, maybe you're right."

Senator Muskie was there, having been summoned to board the plane in Burlington so he could arrive in Air Force One in his home state of Maine. Someone in the White House had come up with this maneuver, which had been followed from state to state on this tour. Muskie was not keen for it, and when we chatted for a few minutes, I told him why I thought it a poor idea.

"When the plane lands and the president comes out, attention is on his meeting the people on the ground, in the reception line," I said. "That's the scene the photographers shoot."

At his podium, LBJ was making sure that he would pick up traditional Republican votes in Vermont as well as the Democratic ones:

> Well, I believe deeply in the Democratic Party. But throughout my career I have worked closely and gained inspiration from Republican colleagues like many of those you have sent to Washington.

Then he put a zinger into Goldwater, indicating that he was no Republican at all:

> One of our great parties had been captured, captured by a faction of men who stand outside the whole range of common agreement and common principles which have brought us to the summit of success. These men have not just marched out of step with American progress—they have refused, and they now refuse to march at all. If they gain control of our government, they would not change the direction of our march; they would just halt it altogether.

There was some more handshaking, and we were in the air again, this time headed for Portland, Maine.

So many cities in which I had been as a harbinger were aggregates of quick impressions: an airport, a hotel, a few streets, a square or plaza, perhaps an auditorium. Portland, Maine, was much more to me. Ol' Doc Johnson's Medicine Show was flying toward the city to which my wife and I had traveled by train thirteen years earlier to begin a ten-year stay in Maine where our youth would be left and our four boys born. We rode the train because we did not have a car. I was to be "manager" of the one-man United Press bureau. We went north of Boston toward Longfellow's town of black wharves and slips and shadowy trees and the graves on Munjoy Hill of the two sea captains whose ships had thundered at each other in Casco Bay, where the islands were scattered like the Hesperides.

As we flew toward Portland, I thought of that earlier arrival by train. We had found remnants of Longfellow's vision.

We lived in a garden apartment on the Back Cove, a weak promise of the sea. By day I covered Maine by telephone from a dingy office downtown, except when I was able to break the shackles of telephone and teletype and at least see what I was writing about. Old news stories ran through my mind. The day I called upon Mrs. Robert Peary, who lived in a nongarden apartment about 200 yards from ours on that backwater. She spoke of being a young wife going north with her husband for the first time, and you could see her standing in the bow with the salt spray on her face. We did not get into the controversy over whether he had actually reached the North Pole. At the end of our talk she became crochety. After giving me what I needed for an anniversary story on her husband's trek to the Pole, she said, "Come back again, but next time don't stay so long."

Her daughter, the "Snow Baby" born in Greenland, let me out.

And then there were the court cases where I sat in on sordid and unmysterious murder trials in which the weapons were butcher knives or washing machine agitators, and the perpetrators had been caught within five minutes. The sameness of the court routine was broken when Dr. Wilhem Reich, a disciple of Sigmund Freud, established his Orgone Institute in Maine and ran afoul of the federal government for selling Orgone boxes, which drew Orgone energy from the skies and which, depending upon their size, could be sat inside or applied to limbs to cure ills ranging from colds to cancer.

Before Reich was haled into federal court, he and/or his associates decided that the publicity had all been bad and that less skeptical accounts were in order. My persistent telephone calls to the institute at Rangeley ("Say, what is Orgone energy?") were answered by unidentified voices, one of them harsh and forceful. The calls led to my being summoned to a private press conference in one of the largest reception rooms of the Eastland Hotel. There was a tiny table in the middle of the floor and two straightbacked chairs. An attendant ushered in Dr. Reich, white-haired, red-faced, bull-like. He came to the table, and we shook hands.

"Sit down," he said, looking me over carefully.

We sat for a moment, and he said, "Are you a learner?"

I thought over what I did for a living and replied "No-o. I'm a conduit."

He stood up.

"Press conference is over."

He strode from the room.

The last time I saw him, he had been sentenced. A deputy marshal was leading him from the courtroom of U.S. District Judge John J. Clifford. At the door, he turned.

"My equations for negative gravity will be lost forever," he shouted.

The door swung shut behind him.

This was the town where I heard an earnest young Democratic lawyer, Edmund S. Muskie, deliver his first speeches as he sought to become governor. The Republican incumbent had some patronizing advice: the struggling Maine Democratic Party should try to win some local offices before setting its sights on the big ones. This was before Muskie's election.

The wooden mansions on the Eastern Promenade looking out to the Maine Hesperides had been cut up into apartments or rooming houses. Back from them on the narrow streets of Munjoy Hill lived the working men holding on in old neighborhoods and the poor living as they could. On one street was the Post Office supervisor with the hearty family who led the city's Great Books program; on another, a twisting alley, the blind couple with the five young children. The father played an accordion on street corners. We went to a party at their house one night, my wife and I doing the serving because we had the only eyes that worked. One of the male guests got up and sang "Beautiful, beautiful brown eyes . . . I'll never love blue eyes again."

The people with money had gone to live on Cape Elizabeth, and in Falmouth Foreside, and Cumberland Foreside, farther and farther out. But they were coming back this night in 1964 to join the downtown people and see the president from Texas. He would speak from the steps of City Hall. It would not be at 5:24 p.m., as the schedule said. It would be more like 7:30 p.m. The trip was running late, and it would be running later. The people of the Portland area were out in full force. Census figures showed a population of 70,000 for Portland. Colonel Robert Marx, Maine State Police chief, estimated that 100,000 persons turned out to see the president. They were at the airport, along the streets into town; they were jammed on both sides of Congress Street and squeezed into City Hall plaza. Bennett Webber, chief of the Portland Police, put the figure somewhere between 50,000 and 75,000. But all such estimates are guesses. The simple fact was that nobody had ever seen such a crowd before in Portland. On an ordinary night, Henry Wadsworth Longfellow's statue was lonely in Longfellow Square on Congress Street. Not this night. He was a boulder in the sea. And, according to my old friend Mickey Wiesenthal, a reporter for the *Portland Press Herald*, who had once worked for the *Brooklyn Eagle* and whose father had been run out of New York and its garment industry by the gangster Lepke, the huge crowd around City Hall had started to gather by 2 p.m.

At the airport, the usual happened. Democratic Senator Edmund Muskie, behind the president and Mrs. Johnson getting off the plane, was upstaged by Republican Governor John H. Reed, who was on the ground to greet the Johnsons. Reed thought that he would do his duty and then be on his way. But Johnson captured him and put him to work, and Reed did not know what to do but oblige. He was a young man, a potato grower and an amateur harness racer from Presque Isle in Maine's northern tip. I had told him he was governor at 3 a.m. on December 31, 1959. I had been asleep in the staff house on the grounds of the Blaine House when the telephone rang. It was the housekeeper from the main house. Governor Clauson was "awful sick," she said.

"Mrs. Clauson wants you to come over."

I dressed quickly and walked across the yard. The governor was in bed. He was dead. I did not need the doctor to tell me that when he arrived. The doctor made an attempt to revive him and I helped, but it was useless. I asked him to get another doctor to join him in pronouncing the governor dead, and he did. Mrs. Clauson was distraught. The married children had to be summoned. The governor's close friends had to be called. I had to tell the press. Bob Crocker, the AP man, asked me if I had told John Reed, president of the Maine State Senate, that he was governor. When I said "not yet," he said that he would wait and talk to Reed after I did. I called Presque Isle. Reed answered the telephone, and I told him what had happened and what he had become. Later he said that when he put down the phone he sat and looked at it for twenty minutes.

This night in Portland he found himself participating in a Democratic campaign.

"Where's the governor?" shouted the president from his car after he had clutched all available hands.

Valenti or someone went after Reed, and he was bundled into the presidential car. Several times when the president hopped out for impromptu orations, he thrust the bullhorn into Reed's hands as well as into the hands of the Democratic candidates. Reed had to say a few words. Later, when he had become chairman of the National Governor's Conference, Johnson continued to hand him the bullhorn, symbolically then, to endorse presidential policies.

I was riding in the rear of the motorcade in an open convertible with Mac Kilduff. People I had known for years in Portland or while at the State House in Augusta kept rushing out to the car to call me by name and shake my hand.

"Hey," said Kilduff finally, "what the hell's this all about?"

I sighed. "Happens all the time. Looks like a groundswell."

Have you noticed the electric unreality of great gatherings at night? The theatricality of lights, the long shadows, the rear of crowds disappearing into the enclosing dark? I was familiar with that strange excitement. I had felt it strongly at Carswell Air Force Base just ten months earlier, when the blue-and-white aircraft dropped out of the night and rolled to the crowd on the airport apron. It was that way in Portland. The old torchlight parades must have generated the same kind of excitement, probably heightened by the flickering of the torches.

Longfellow Square. Congress Square. Monument Square. The motorcade crept toward City Hall. The automobiles finally pulled up to its side and the passengers got out and went to the front steps. I went directly to one of our telephones behind the platform and talked to Warren O'Donnell in Manchester, New Hampshire, the next stop.

"Where the hell are you?" said Warren.

"Portland. Still a-comin'."

He gave me some last-minute names for the president to mention when he reached Manchester, and I had them typed in a City Hall room by one of the secretaries from Senator Muskie's office.

Out front, Lyndon Johnson was speaking exuberantly. He had introduced Lady Bird as "my sweetheart," and she had spoken briefly and graciously, praising New England's fall foliage and the welcome the people had given her husband. Then LBJ was off in full swing, the president of all the people, the preacher at a political rally that somehow was to be both partisan and nonpartisan. Republican votes were as good as Democratic votes. After some extravagant praise for May Craig, Washington correspondent for the Guy Gannett Newspapers of Maine, Ed Muskie received a presidential accolade as "able, fearless, diligent, courageous." William D. Hathaway and Kenneth

Curtis were mentioned in the introduction but then became nameless "fine Democratic candidates for Congress." Margaret Chase Smith, who was not present and whose Senate seat was not at stake, was "your own great Republican senator." And part of the team that was going to put Maine on the map economically was "the governor of this state," John Reed, whose office was not being voted on in 1964. Unity was the thing.

"The greatness of this Nation rests on the unity of its people."

And they could demonstrate that greatness by uniting behind Lyndon Baines Johnson.

This same Lyndon Baines Johnson was going to "call up Sargent Shriver and tell him to get in touch with Ed Muskie and the governor" and do something right away for Maine under the new Economic Opportunities Act when LBJ got back to Washington. And, of course, "Lyndon Baines Johnson is going to do something about Passamaquoddy," and all good Republicans and Democrats were going to help him. The "something," which he should not have let drop, was to be another report on the proposed tidal power project. On and on he went in great gyres.

My attention wandered to Adam Walsh, who had introduced the president. Adam had been a minority leader in the Maine House of Representatives and before that had coached Bowdoin College football teams for many years and before that had been center on Notre Dame's Four Horsemen team. Now he was U.S. marshal for Maine, thanks to the Democratic presidential victory in 1960. He had come within a heartbeat of being named earlier Maine's fish and game commissioner. I had handled Governor Clauson's appointments to office, and in my book for posting the week that the governor died was the name of Adam Walsh for the fish and game position. It was never posted.

Suddenly the talking was over, and there was a rush to the cars. The crowd was excited and boisterous, and for a few minutes the automobiles were imbedded in the masses of people. Secret Service agents and police began pushing back the crowd. I joined in to help and found myself hand in hand with a plainclothesman whose face was familiar. He looked at me, puzzled, but we ended up just nodding heads as the motorcade began to move. I swung over the back door of the last convertible and looked back as the cars gathered speed. Captain Edward Kochian, that was his name. Last time I had seen him the newsmen were waiting around the Portland Police Station for information about the investigation of a Christmas season death. A woman's body had been found by the Christmas creche in Evergreen Cemetery. She had been picked up in a barroom by a guy and thrown out in the cold where she died of exposure. The woman's husband was brought into the police station from his laboring job, and Kochian told him of his wife's death, and its circumstances. The husband, his face grimy from his work, wiped his eyes.

He looked across at the waiting newsmen.

"She was all right." he said. "Don't be hard on her."

We drove back to the airport by a different route, passing what was left of Longfellow's Deering Woods.

There was a good crowd at the airport. People who could not get close to City Hall had gone to the airport fences. When the motorcade was rolling down the apron, I heard my name through the roar. Art and Jan Perrin and their blond children were at the front of the crowd. I jumped from the car and ran back. We talked about the years since they had lived above us in the garden apartments on the Back Cove. Now their home was a restored 200-year-old farmhouse in North Windham. I ran for the press plane and climbed aboard, just in time.

The Presidential Campaign Special was running three hours late when it set down at the airport in Manchester, New Hampshire. Despite the long wait in the dark, the crowds at the airport and along the streets were strong. The activities were to take place at Bill Dunfey's Carpenter Motor Inn, so the motorcade drove directly there. At one point, however, LBJ had time to stop and climb atop a white Lincoln with bullhorn in hand, the arms of Secret Servicemen supporting him like flying buttresses.

One of the extra advance men I had sent to Warren O'Donnell from Washington was in line with a reception group waiting to shake the president's hand.

"What's with him?" I asked Warren whom I found to be a shorter and stockier man than his older brother, Ken.

Warren shook his head.

"Some of the guys you send along are beauts."

I talked with Bill Dunfey, long one of New Hampshire's leading Democrats, and ate some of his food while the Manchester program started. Later I went to the room where the president was addressing members of the New Hampshire Weekly Newspaper Editors

Association. The room was packed, so I listened at the door for a while and then took a break. I should have paid attention. Reading that speech later was to recognize a remarkable performance. It was a popular primer of LBJ's approach to foreign policy, among other things. He was proud of huge expenditures for defense. He invoked the names of President Eisenhower, John Foster Dulles, Arthur Vandenburg, and Warren Austin to go along with a string of Democratic names in support of a bipartisan foreign policy. He talked about halting Communist aggression in Greece and Turkey and Korea and the Formosa Straits, in Cuba, and in the Gulf of Tonkin. When he dug into Vietnam, he said:

> So just for the moment I have not thought that we were ready for American boys to do the fighting for Asian boys. What I have been trying to do, with the situation that I found, was to get the boys in Vietnam to do their own fighting with our advice and with our equipment. That is the course we are following. So we are not going north and drop bombs at this stage of the game, and we are not going south and run out and leave it for the Communists to take over.

I guess the key words were "for the moment" and "at this stage of the game."

Later, many would read and ponder those and other words of his speech. I know I did. They provided indications of the course that the United States would follow in the Vietnam War while Lyndon Johnson was commander in chief. The generation of allied victors in World War II tended to look on world affairs with a certain truculence along with remedial action, such as the establishment of the United Nations and the Marshall Plan. Although John Kennedy's inaugural address was justifiably hailed for its eloquence, there was a trace in it of muscle-flexing. I am thinking particularly of this passage:

> Let every nation know, whether it wishes us well or ill, that we shall pay any price, bear any burden, meet any hardship, support any friend, oppose any foe to assure the survival and the success of liberty.

Triumphalism, born of the justifiable World War II?

Noticeable in LBJ's talk to the New Hampshire editors was a reference to the recent provocative action against a U.S. destroyer in the Gulf of Tonkin and the American retaliation. The president would later justify increased American participation in the Vietnam War on the basis of that confused incident.

There is another part of that New Hampshire speech that struck me as revealing about LBJ's state of mind at the time and, probably, as characteristic of the man:

> One of our old cow puncher friends took some cattle up to Kansas City to sell, and one of the fellows out in the stockyards said to him, while they were waiting for the bidder to come in, "Please tell me what is the difference between a Sheriff and a Texas Ranger." The old man, a Ranger for many years, ran his hand through his hair and deliberated, and he said, "Well a Ranger is one when you plug him, when you hit him, he just keeps coming." And we must let the rest of the world know that we speak softly, we carry a big stick, but we have the will and the determination, and if they ever hit us it is not going to stop—we are just going to keep coming.

I expected large numbers of "American boys" to serve eventually in Vietnam, but not 500,000.

He had an amusing and a favorite anecdote about the youngster who left his cotton patch to hear U.S. Senator Joseph Weldon Bailey talk for nearly half a day, and when asked by his employer what the senator said, he replied:

> Boss, I don't remember. I don't recollect precisely what the senator said, but the general impression I got was the senator was recommending himself most highly!

Lyndon Baines Johnson went on to recommend himself most highly as a cool and skillful negotiator in a dangerous world, "president of all the people instead of any single group," careful analyzer and cutter of budgets, and the man who could lead the way to "a prosperous nation, a proud nation, a peaceful nation." Some of the newspaper editors to whom I spoke at the conclusion of the speech were greatly impressed by his performance that night. I wondered if they, and he, realized its implications.

Back to the airport again and into the planes and into the air for Logan International Airport in Boston. The hell with any more running around, I said to myself as we landed in Boston. Besides, this is just supposed to be an unscheduled call on Teddy Kennedy at the hospital, even though it has been on the last three drafts of the schedule. I sank back into my seat in the press plane and went to sleep, awakening when it was time to take off for Washington. Somebody told me that the last they saw of the president he was standing atop an automobile on Boston's Tremont Street haranguing a small crowd at about 2 a.m. He was not going to lose a vote if he could help it. We flew to Washington's National Airport and went home, and the 1964 New England Marathon was over, an amazing test of a candidate's endurance and a clear indication, if you could believe your eyes, of the landslide that was in the making.

CHAPTER 6

Wooing the Wests, Mid and Far

The theory that Lyndon Johnson has extra glands is made almost credible by the fact that on September 29, 1964, the same day that he arrived back at the White House at 4:22 a.m. after exhausting the populace of New England, he went to Omaha, Nebraska. Following a White House luncheon for Secretary General Manlio Brosio of the North Atlantic Treaty Organization (NATO), the president, a thoughtful host, ran his guest out to Omaha after lunch to look at the headquarters of the Strategic Air Command (SAC). There are some, of course, who might think that part of his concern could have been for the voter who, heretofore, might not have been sufficiently aware of Lyndon Johnson's commitment to a mighty aerial striking force in a community of nations not to be trusted fully. The president spoke to the crowd that greeted him at Offutt Air Force Base, and he spoke again outside of SAC headquarters following an inspection and a briefing. General Curtis E. LeMay, chief of staff of the Air Force and later to be George Wallace's running mate, joined General Thomas S. Power, SAC's commander in chief, for the briefing session.

The president was at home on September 30, but on October 1 he went to Baltimore at the invitation of President Milton Eisenhower of Johns Hopkins University to speak to the students and faculty. Marty Underwood had gone to Baltimore earlier as the advance man and reported excellent cooperation from Dr. Eisenhower, the former president's brother. There was little doubt where the younger Eisenhower stood in the presidential campaign.

For the next few days the president was engaged in a flurry of activity at home and was preparing for an assault on the West. I was back on the advance desk, where we were trying to get our people out ahead of him. Before he left on the week-long trip, LBJ gave Mrs. Johnson two send-offs on her whistlestop trip through the

South. She was to travel some 1,600 miles by train to New Orleans, making what turned out to be forty-seven stops in four days. Mrs. Johnson had her own advance crew, and our participation was slight. At Wilson McCarthy's prompting, I went to the railroad station at Alexandria, Virginia, and asked the local politicos who were handling arrangements for the departure ceremony to run through the scenario for me, although they had been working directly with Mrs. Johnson's people. McCarthy wanted a review from the president's standpoint. So I made it.

Early on the morning of October 6, the president said good-bye to his wife and daughter, Lynda, at Alexandria's railroad station as they boarded the "Lady Bird Special" for the campaign trip. And that night he flew down to overtake them at Raleigh, North Carolina, to give them a second send-off at North Carolina State College. Mrs. Johnson noted then that she had made fourteen speeches since she had seen him last.

The president then made his big push through the Midwest and Far West, plane hopping, of course. From October 7 to October 12, my notes show that the schedule went like this:

Des Moines, Iowa	October 7
Springfield, Illinois	7
Peoria, Illinois	7
Chicago, Illinois	7–8
Gary, Indiana	8
Indianapolis, Indiana	8
Cleveland, Ohio	8
Louisville, Kentucky	8–9
Nashville, Tennessee	9
New Orleans, Louisiana (where he met the "Lady Bird Special")	9
Johnson City, Texas (not exactly a campaign stop)	10-11
Phoenix, Arizona	11
Long Beach, California	11
San Francisco, California	11
Las Vegas, Nevada	11–12

Reno, Nevada	12
Butte, Montana	12
Casper, Wyoming	12
Denver, Colorado	12
Boise, Idaho	12

The doors of our quarters in the Democratic National Committee suite, your heart's private information notwithstanding, were swinging in those hectic days. And some of our best advance men were not even checking in but were being routed from stop to stop.

In the midst of this activity, I climbed aboard a plane and went to San Francisco to be the advance man for the October 11th stop there, taking along one new advance man. After seeing Dick Swig, the general manager, we moved into tower rooms in the Fairmount Hotel. Looking at the Bay and the San Francisco hills from my window, I was reminded once again of somebody's observation to the effect that San Francisco and New York were cities with identities, and the rest of the cities were Cleveland. But how did New York get in such good company?

The format of the president's visit to San Francisco this time was to be simple. San Francisco would have its Columbus Day parade on Sunday, October 11, starting at City Hall and winding through the city to Washington Square in the predominantly Italian North Beach. President Johnson would arrive at the tail end of the parade and speak from the reviewing stand in Washington Square. There could hardly be an occasion for a better crowd in San Francisco's Italian section.

As soon as I was in the Fairmount, I got in touch with Mayor John F. Shelley and Tom Saunders of the Democratic Central Committee, and we scheduled meetings. Then, with Secret Service agents from the White House detail and the San Francisco office and the new advance man, Dick Braun, I went to look at Washington Square. Its most striking feature was the huge, towered front of Saints Peter and Paul Church across Filbert Street on the north side. The reviewing stand and bleachers were being erected along the street in front of the church in accordance with what I was told was usual procedure for the parade. This posed a problem. If the president spoke from the reviewing stand, then he would have his back to the park that, anyhow, was rimmed with tall bushes on that side. We could run a catwalk through the bushes and build a new speaking platform for him into the park, but this would cut him off from the people on the reviewing stand and in the reserved seats. The better alternative, it seemed to me, would be to move the reviewing stand to a triangular island at the southwest corner of the park and erect the bleachers alongside it. The parade would be able to pass in front. When it came time for the president to speak, those on the reviewing stand, in the bleachers, and in the huge crowd that I expected in the rising amphitheater of the park would be able to see as well as to hear him.

At a meeting in the mayor's office, Shelley and the parade officials agreed to the change, despite the fact that it meant interrupting busy public transportation at the location that I had selected, not only during the parade but also from the time the carpentry started until the structures could be removed. I gave the word to go ahead. But then Wilson McCarthy jetted into town on a survey and turned me around, a decision that I took with the poorest possible grace. When I showed him the Square, the broad, white face of the church enchanted him.

"A perfect backdrop for photos," he said, adding something about all the bad publicity the Bobby Baker case had caused recently.

"Maybe there could be some priests and nuns waving from up there," he said, gesturing toward the belfry. He may have been joking—probably was.

I reacted with a dirty word to his proposal, objecting, for several reasons, to giving up my plan. But McCarthy wanted that backdrop. So we ordered a catwalk from the reviewing stand through the bushes, with a speaking platform on the end. Although the public address system would permit those in the reviewing stand and the bleachers along the end of the parade route to hear the president, people would not be able to see him, but the church would be behind him.

I imagined what *The Sun Herald* would have said about such a photographic prop. In the fall of 1950, I had joined a group of young people in Kansas City where, in a store rented from Fibber McGee's brother on the ragtag end of 12th Street, we began to publish a five-day-a-week national and local Catholic newspaper. *The Sun Herald* said it hoped to present the news in the light of Christian values. My participation was motivated by a measure of zeal and the prospect of marrying the red-haired girl I had met in journalism college and who had already joined the newspaper. Staffers lived in voluntary poverty in the midst of taverns with hillbilly bands and storefronts emblazoned with "Bail Bonds" and published the paper for seven months, distributing it to some 10,000 subscribers, before the economics of publishing newspapers caught up with us and the store went back to Fibber McGee's brother and the staff scattered across the country. I returned to the United Press.

Workmen quickly hammered together the catwalk and speaking platform in the park of San Francisco's Washington Square. Tom Saunders and his associates in charge of the Democratic Party apparatus performed their tasks with professional competence, making the advance man's job comparatively easy. They mobilized the various committees, checked on what they were doing, distributed campaign materials, said the right things to the press, and did not push private campaign projects. At the appropriate time, they even tacked up on telephone poles the circular "LBJ Route" signs that I carried in my bag. I was able to devote some of my own time to what had become a favorite pastime: riding the cable cars around San Francisco.

In the meantime, I worked up a schedule. LBJ would arrive at San Francisco airport at 3:30 p.m., would depart by high-speed motorcade up the freeway at 3:35, and would enter Washington Square at 4:05 at the end of the Columbus Day parade. After a few words by others and the usual introductions, he would begin speaking at 4:20, finish his talk at 4:40, and, after some handshaking, he would be on his way from the Square at 4:50 p.m. From long experience, of course, I knew these times were imaginary.

Angier Biddle Duke and Chet Carter of the Department of State's Protocol Office began to ring me on the telephone, and a new element was introduced. President Diosdada Macapagal of the Philippines and his wife had been in Washington on a state visit during the week preceding the San Francisco stop, and they would be in San Francisco at the same time as the president. So, although President Johnson had been their host in Washington, arrangements were made for him to pay a courtesy call to them at the Fairmount Hotel before departing from San Francisco. I made these additions to the schedule:

5 p.m.   Arrive Fairmount for meeting with Macapagal
5:20 p.m.   Depart for airport
5.50 p.m.   Arrive San Francisco airport
6 p.m.   Wheels up

Then I met with the Italian leaders and agreed on a program that I checked out with the mayor. Joseph Manette, president of the Columbus Celebration Committee, would open the speaking program and introduce Father Joseph Costanzo, who would deliver the invocation. After the prayer, Manette would introduce John Ertola, chairman of the City Columbus Day Committee. Ertola would introduce Mayor Shelley, who would introduce Democratic Congressmen Philip Burton of San Francisco and Peter W. Rodino Jr. of New Jersey, who would be along for obvious reasons. Shelley also would introduce Senator Pierre Salinger, who had been appointed to the Senate seat of the late Clair Engle of California and was a candidate to retain that seat in the election, Italian ambassador to the United States, Sergio Fenoalta, and Governor Edmund G. (Pat) Brown of California. Brown would introduce the president. After a while, you become adept at such Tinkers-to-Evers-to-Chance arrangements.

I wrote in my pocket notebook that the Secret Service should lay on an open Lincoln, and a closed one for the president and Secret Service to switch to when appropriate, a staff car, a VIP car, three convertibles and a closed car for the press, and a car for the White House Communications Agency. In addition, my note reminded me, I was to arrange for three press buses.

Two days before the president was due to arrive, his Republican opponent, Senator Barry Goldwater, came to San Francisco to speak at Fisherman's Wharf. I was busy and did not go. The newspapers said that 7,500 persons attended the nighttime address, and that Goldwater told the crowd that Christopher Columbus, whom he had enlisted as a Republican, was "an individualist," and that if he "were around today somebody might call him an extremist." The size of the crowd heartened me.

Another item in the newspapers made me feel proud of our man. President Johnson was in New Orleans on October 9, after a hard day of campaigning, to meet the "Lady Bird Special" and then to speak at a fund-raising dinner. In that speech, although he was in segregation territory and his host, Governor John J. McKeithan, on the back of the platform was not endorsing his candidacy, Johnson gave it to his audience straight about "the law of the land," and everybody who heard him knew what he was talking about: the Civil Rights Act. He said forthrightly to his Louisiana audience:

I signed it, and I am going to observe it, and I think any man that is worthy of the high office of president is going to do the same thing.

And then, in his inimitable way of storytelling, he let the segregationists have it between the eyes. It was a story about an old Texas political leader who had left his own unidentified Southern state to settle in Texas but wanted to go back to his old state "and make them one more Democratic speech. . . . The poor old State, they haven't heard a Democratic speech in thirty years. All they ever hear at election time is Negro, Negro, Negro!"

That made good reading while we were waiting.

The president left the ranch early on Sunday, April 11, and ran up to Phoenix, Arizona, Barry Goldwater's hometown, to go to church with Roy L. Elson, Democratic candidate for the seat being vacated by old Senator Carl Hayden of Arizona. ("This is not a day for politics. This is a day for God, and since this is God's day I will leave very shortly [from the Phoenix airport] and go with my old and longtime friend, Roy Elson, down to hear his preacher.") From church, LBJ flew to Long Beach, California, for a speech in Municipal Park at South Gate, about a dozen miles from the Long Beach Airport, a route that I heard by telephone from our man down there was lined with enormous crowds. And then the president was to fly to San Francisco, where we waited. We waited a long time. Lyndon Johnson was not one to give up a crowd in the hand.

I spent some time in Washington Square convincing the police that the ropes and stanchions to keep the crowd at bay were too far from the platform and should be pulled in tighter. Then I talked with Joe Cervetto, who was decked out as Columbus, and Angela Giammona, who was costumed as Queen Isabella. As the afternoon wore on, a telephone at the platform rang, and Major General Chester V. Clifton, the president's military aide, was on the line from Southern California. Since the presidential party was running so late, said Clifton, what did I think of the possibility of the president skipping San Francisco and flying directly to Las Vegas, which was the next stop? The president had been to San Francisco, and everybody loved him there. I told him what I thought. I thought I should be talking to Bill Moyers or anybody else who knew something about politics.

He got Moyers for me, and we talked for a few minutes, and Moyers said, "Hang on, we're coming."

The parade ended as we waited, and the grassy square filled up as more and more spectators who had been watching the parade elsewhere came to hear the president. We had Julie Andrews and Dick Van Dyke on the platform, and Van Dyke was prevailed upon to do some clowning to help pass the time. I pulled out and went to the airport to do my waiting there, leaving the new advance man at the Square.

I had called Congressman Burton, who was in his San Francisco office, a couple of days earlier and invited him to the airport to ride in the motorcade to Washington Square. While I was waiting for Air Force One, Burton came up, looked at the president's limousine, and said, "So this is what we'll be riding in."

I told him "no," that he would be riding in the VIP car, car number 2. In the first car, I said, would be the president, Governor Brown, Senator Salinger, Mayor Shelley, and Ambassador Fenoalta. That meant three in the back seat and two on the jump seats. A Secret Service agent would be riding up front with the driver. Radio equipment wiped out the middle seat in the front.

"Wait a minute," he said. "Wilson McCarthy promised me I would get everything that the mayor gets on this trip." Burton and Shelley were not friends.

"The mayor is the host," I said. "He has to ride in the car. There are no more seats, so we have no choice."

"I am riding in this car," said Burton, a big man. Standing between him and the limousine, I said, "You will have to come through me to do it."

We hung around the black car like jealous matadors, and then he drifted off. Soon Air Force One was in the sky, then on the ground. I went to the ramp as the presidential party emerged.

The president said to Shelley "Have you got any Italians for me today?"

"We have a few," replied the mayor.

The president was in a hurry and headed to his car, shepherding his guests. The president climbed in and Congressman Burton climbed in. The president snapped on the loudspeaker system and growled into a microphone, "Come on. Let's get going."

Salinger got in. Shelley got in. Fenoalta got in.

There were no more seats. Governor Brown walked around the car and said, "Say, where do I sit?"

I opened the back door and assisted/pushed the governor of California onto the jump seat, upon which the Italian ambassador already was sitting.

As I shut the door, I murmured, "You'll each have to ride on one cheek." The motorcade started, and I ran to get aboard at the rear.

The plane had touched down at 4:50 p.m., one hour and twenty minutes after the time sanguinely listed on the schedule. The motorcade raced north on the freeway behind a phalanx of fifty motorcycles, slowing to crowd speed after exiting from the freeway. The streets approaching Washington Square were deeply lined with people. The Square itself had blossomed during my absence. Police Chief Thomas J. Cahill estimated that 100,000 persons were packed there, a good round number. LBJ began his shenanigans, including forays into the crowds and the tottering-on-the-car act. He pulled Pierre Salinger up on the trunk of the car with him.

The president shook hands through the reviewing stand and into the bleachers. Then he walked across the catwalk through the bushes for the speaking program. Before it started, his "elbow men," Secret Service agents Rufus Youngblood and Lem Johns, finally quieted down a rambunctious group of young people at a back corner of the platform by the bushes. I ran over the program quickly with the platform guests, and the speaking started. When it was Governor Brown's turn, he introduced the president and forgot what I had told him about the lectern. LBJ was known to get excitable when the lectern was not four feet high. We had one of those up and down lecterns that was down to accommodate those among the speakers who were short in stature. Brown was to hit the button at the end of his introduction, and the electrically powered lectern would rise to the proper height for the president. But the governor just moved back after the introduction. The president stepped forward, staring down at the lectern. I slipped in front of him and pressed the button, and the lectern came riding up to the right height. Small things could become big things with Lyndon Johnson. You had better be sure that the lectern was at the proper height, and you had better oversee the erecting of the photographers' platform so that it was forty-five degrees off to his left.

As the president began to speak on the wind-buffeted platform and the photographers made their pictures, I looked back at the huge face of the church with its twin towers behind him. There were no priests and nuns waving from the belfry. A pair of policemen stood up there.

The speech was not memorable, but it received rousing cheers, and the president mixed jovially with the crowd on the way to his car. The motorcade went to the Fairmount for the president's visit with President Macapagal. LBJ noticed a cocktail party of the Ironworkers District Council while he was in the hotel and dropped in unannounced to shake some hands. Then we went to the ships, the airships. The president embarrassed a young Air Force sergeant at the foot of the plane stairs by making him break out of his rigid salute for a handshake.

"Aw, come on now, son. Shake hands with the president."

Then Air Force One whisked down the runway and into the air. It was 6:50 p.m. The plane was headed for Nevada. Lyndon Johnson's Sunday, which began in church, was to end in Las Vegas following the two intermediate stops in California. John Bunyan could have made something of that.

Back at my tower room, I looked at some pills that had been prescribed by a hotel doctor two days earlier for hoarseness or laryngitis or whatever it was that had dropped my voice to a scratchy echo. I put them away and took a half-used bottle of Black and White Scotch from the bathroom and sat in front of the window with a glass, looking out at San Francisco and beyond. Wilson McCarthy called in the morning and said I should meet him in New York City, where the president would be on October 14–15, in addition to making a few side trips. So I went there.

CHAPTER 7

A Little Rally in a Big Place

New York is a suburb of Larchmont to me. Larchmont is where I grew up, when the developers had not pushed the houses so far into the woods around the reservoir and when Long Island Sound tumbled brightly around you as you clung to a line from the stern of a Snipe on a windy day. In bicycle reach by quiet roads were Kensico Dam and Byram Lake and, nearer, Orienta Point, where among the big lawns there was a fine haunted house with sightless windows and a widow's walk, and Edgewater Point, where the tan grasses waved like the water. When I go to New York, I go first to Larchmont, even though the destructives have rammed the monstrous New England Thruway through the old railroad station and the park, where there was a pond and trees and flowers, so everybody can race like hell to places no longer worth seeing.

Arriving by air from San Francisco with a hoarse throat, a soiled trenchcoat, and a scuffed suitcase and plaid fabric two-suiter, both of them filled with dirty clothes mixed with campaign materials, I took a cab from the airport to 125th Street and caught the New Haven. The train fell victim to some unspecified malady outside the Mt. Vernon or New Rochelle station for about an hour. The delay was rendered pleasant by the appearance of a classmate from high school days at Iona, Al Hoffmann, who had since become the father of many girls and a vice president of BBD&O, the advertising agency. Al had been sitting a few seats back and because of the passage of a score of years had not been sure for a while about the identity of the travel-worn drummer up front. We were able to recap the years before the wheels resumed rolling and deposited him at New Rochelle. I got off at Larchmont and spent the night and next morning with my parents before returning to the campaign, refreshed in spirit and attire.

Warren O'Donnell was the advance man for the New York stop. I checked into his quarters at the Carlisle Hotel, where he was sharing a suite with Bernie Boutin and Bill Dunfey of New Hampshire. Nobody was home, so I went in search of McCarthy. Being well met, we stopped for a shine, at his instigation, and then proceeded to Democratic headquarters and discovered that the party's arrangements for the president's visit were not at the polished stage, because even the factions have factions in New York Democratic politics.

If I were writing a play about the 1964 campaign, I would set the New York events of October 14–15 in a suite that we used as our headquarters in the Waldorf-Astoria Hotel. The action and dialog would provide a sidelong rather than a headlong look at the events. That, of course, was my view of President Johnson throughout the campaign.

O'Donnell was harried, but he seemed to be doing all right under New York circumstances, coping with the various Democratic committees, with the prima donnas of the city's congressional delegation, and with Brooklyn Leader Stanley Steingut and Johnson's old associate, Edwin L. Weisl, and Edwin Weisl Jr. Because he was dealing with so many people, Warren got nabbed by a reporter for the *New York Times*. A sidebar in the October 14 *Times* on the presidential visit began:

> The most sought-after political figure in New York this week was a 33 year-old Worcester, Mass., businessman. He is Warren O'Donnell, President Johnson's advance man for the president's visit to the state today and tomorrow.

Buried in the story was this sentence:

> He wears a gold tie-clip shaped in the form of New York State with "Kennedy '64" stamped on it, referring to the senatorial campaign of Robert F. Kennedy.

I never heard if President Johnson saw or reacted to that detail.

The president was to campaign in Bergen, New Jersey, and the Wilkes Barre-Scranton area of Pennsylvania on Wednesday, October 14, and then speak at the Annual Dinner of the Alfred E. Smith Memorial Foundation at the Waldorf-Astoria that night. Francis Cardinal Spellman made the selection of a speaker, and the choice of Johnson so close to the election appeared significant. On Thursday,

October 15, Johnson would visit Rochester and Buffalo, New York, with Robert F. Kennedy, and in the late afternoon there would be a circuit tour of Brooklyn. The president would speak at a Liberal Party rally in Madison Square Garden Thursday night and after the rally would return to Washington.

On Wednesday, looking ahead to the following day while we waited for the president, McCarthy had the idea that I should be in a police car a mile ahead of the motorcade on Thursday to check each of the stops as the president and his entourage of New York politicians traveled through Brooklyn. He asked Walter B. Coleman, deputy commissioner of the city's Marine-Aviation Department, who was with us, to make the arrangements. Coleman was dubious.

"You don't know the New York Police department." McCarthy gave him hell. He was not used to anyone saying "no" or even "maybe" to a representative of the White House.

Coleman made the request to the police. When I checked on it later, a detective on the desk said offhandedly, "That's been turned down. We don't do things like that in New York."

I made no appeal up the line. How much good could I do a mile in front of the motorcade anyhow? The arrangements for the two days were in fair enough shape by now. I dropped out of sight until it was time to go to LaGuardia Airport and prepare for the president's arrival. When it was time, we went out and brought him back. He paid a quiet call to Mrs. Jacqueline Kennedy in her Park Avenue apartment. Later, around his suite in the Waldorf Towers, you could feel the trouble in the air. The Walter Jenkins story was breaking in Washington.

I had a drink with Mac Kilduff in the Waldorf bar. At the suggestion of one of the hotel managers, some of us went into the grill and ate double lamb chops, I, at least, under the impression that the manager was picking up the tab. This was an unfounded assumption. I guess he just said that the double lamb chops were good. They were certainly expensive.

McCarthy, Warren O'Donnell, and I went up to the presidential suite. The president was behind closed doors with the Jenkins problem and with a hoarse throat. It had become common knowledge that Jenkins, Johnson's longtime and close aide, had been arrested in the Washington YMCA near the White House a week earlier on a morals charge, and that there had been a similar arrest in 1959. The press was asking questions.

We sat and talked with Robert Kennedy and Ethel Kennedy in a side room of the president's suite while a doctor was summoned to relieve LBJ's throat difficulty. Listening to my croak imported from San Francisco, Ethel Kennedy suggested that the doctor should see me rather than the president. As we were passing the time, I recalled to Robert Kennedy the last time we had talked. It had been in Augusta, Maine, the day of Governor Clauson's funeral, January 2, 1960.

He nodded. "I remember."

It also was the day that John F. Kennedy announced his candidacy for the Democratic nomination for president at a press conference in Washington. Robert Kennedy had flown to Maine from Massachusetts in a light plane to represent his brother at the funeral. He was standing in the Blaine House looking lost in a room of crying women when I walked in. Someone told me that he had been looking for me. I went over to him, and he almost jumped at me in relief.

I had been making the arrangements for the funeral, which was to be held in the Augusta armory, the largest building in town, to accommodate everyone who wanted to be there. Bobby Kennedy rode with me and my wife and the other governor's aide, Maurice F. Williams, and his wife. The five of us sat with the family at Mrs. Clauson's request. Bobby wanted to ride with us to the burial at Pine Grove Cemetery in Waterville, the little city where the governor had lived. But Kennedy had a problem. The pilot whose plane was at the Waterville airport had no navigational aids and had to get back to Massachusetts before dark. So Kennedy wanted us to peel off from the funeral cortege just before the cemetery and take him to the airport. He was insistent. He wanted to ride with us.

I could appreciate his position. He had not known the governor but was representing his brother who had known him. He wanted to be seen with those who had been close to the governor. But I could not agree to leaving the procession.

"Look," I said as we stood outside the armory while the cars pulled into position behind the hearse, "I'll get you a car and you ride behind us and cut out when you have to."

I called to a National Guard officer and had him bring up a car with a driver. Kennedy obviously did not care for the arrangements, but he shook hands and got into the car, which left the procession at the turnoff for the Waterville airport.

In 1964, in the Waldorf, October 14 dragged on. The doctor came and went. I left the president's suite to go downstairs to the banquet room where the Smith dinner was being held. I rode down in the tower elevator with George E. Reedy, the president's press secretary, who was shaking his shaggy white head all the way down.

"I get all the dirty jobs," he said.

He was on his way to meet the press, where he would have to confirm the story about Walter Jenkins and announce Jenkins's resignation from the White House staff. He had known Jenkins for a long time. I saw him talking to the reporters, but I did not linger. I went to the Smith dinner.

There were 2,000 people in the banquet hall to hear the speeches at the Alfred E. Smith Memorial Dinner. I sat for a while at the table where my brother, Monsignor Harry J. Byrne, was a guest. I also stopped to talk with a priest at another table, Monsignor Terence Cooke, later to become Cardinal Cooke. When I knew him in pre-World War II days, he was Terry Cooke, a tall seminarian with black, bushy hair, serving as head counselor of the Badger Day Camp in Westchester County, where I was a junior counselor.

President Johnson spoke late. It was after 11:15 p.m. when he began his remarks, looking and sounding tired. The strain of the Jenkins case showed. Usually the sight of an audience would cause him to throw off evidences of fatigue, despite the most exhausting schedule. He cut short his address, explaining that:

I have prepared a statement somewhat more lengthy than I think would be appropriate to give at this late hour, but I shall try to hit the high points, and I stand upon everything in the somewhat fuller exposition.

It was not a night for presidential speech making. The next morning he and Bobby Kennedy went campaigning in upstate New York and the crowds, we were told when the party came back, were as good as ever. Some of us had stayed in the Waldorf to work on the New York City activities set for later in the day.

If the president had not been revived by his receptions in Rochester and Buffalo, then the borough of Brooklyn would have done that on its own. To a Lyndon Johnson watcher at this stage of the campaign, only two kinds of crowds could surprise: sparse crowds or heaped-up-and-running-over crowds. I never saw the first kind, but the second kind was all over the twenty-two miles of the Brooklyn motorcade route. Lyndon Johnson was up on top of the car,

Kennedy was up, the congressman whose district it was was handed up. The crowds shouted and cheered. At Albee Square, the site of the major rally, there was almost as much excitement as the day when the Dodgers who then called Brooklyn their home beat the Yankees in the 1955 World Series. At one intersection, the president of the United States beckoned to the New York police to let the people come through the barricades, which they were straining against. The police refused. I grinned.

That night I went over to Madison Square Garden to check out final arrangements for the president's speech at a Liberal Party rally that was to be televised. One of the Secret Service agents, an old hand, came up to me and said, "Hey, the band leader here is counting on playing 'Hail to the Chief' when the president shows up. Don't you think you should give him a clue?"

I told the leader to make it "Hello, Lyndon" to the tune of "Hello Dolly."

When the president arrived, I met him at the door and led him through the corridors to the platform. He was communicative, mentioning the day's crowds and asking about the timing of the night's program. I told him that he was cutting the time a little thin because the Liberals had a paid TV schedule that had to be met. After I left him on the platform, a network technician volunteered that my $3.19 pocketwatch, which I was wont to flourish like a Swiss chronometer to get things moving, was four minutes fast.

There were 20,000 enthusiastic people on hand in the Garden. While the speech making was going on, I took a look outside the side door on 49th Street, where some enthusiasts had rigged a makeshift platform so that the president could address a few thousand more people waiting outside the Garden. Secret Service agents indicated opposition. They were apprehensive, particularly about the dark building across the street. After huddling with McCarthy and others, it was decided that I should lead the president back to his car, ignoring the unscheduled event.

Accompanied by his agents, he followed me from the platform at the end of the program but stopped short after a few steps down a corridor toward his car. "Where's the little rally?" he asked loudly. "I want to go to the little rally."

I had not known that he knew about it. Someone had primed him. There was nothing to do but reverse direction and go to the "little rally" on 49th Street. Although he had been face-to-face with mammoth crowds all day long, Lyndon Johnson was not overlooking a vote. He spoke to the small gathering on the side street before returning to Washington.

.

CHAPTER 8

The End of the Affair

In the seventeen days that were left in the campaign, Lyndon Johnson visited cities and towns from one end of the country to the other. I sat in our office in Washington dispatching and supervising advance men. The best of them were on the go constantly, and this led to a wives' revolt. Two young advance men who had proven to be adept operators balked one night as I tried by telephone to shift them from a completed stop to a stop in another city.

"Hey," I asked, "how come?"

"Because," said the one on the phone, "our wives gave us an ultimatum. 'Come home, or else . . .' "

They returned to their homes in the Washington area but were out on the road again in a few days.

From the two-day stay in New York City to the end of the campaign, the schedule went like this:

Cincinnati, Ohio	October 16
Dayton, Ohio	16
Akron, Ohio	21
St. Louis, Missouri	21
Belleville, Illinois	21
East St. Louis, Illinois	21
New York City (funeral services for President Hoover)	22
Memphis, Tennessee	24
Chattanooga, Tennessee	24

Baltimore, Maryland	24
Ft. Lauderdale, Florida	25
Boca Raton, Florida	25
Miami, Florida	25–26
Orlando, Florida	25–26
Jacksonville, Florida	26
Macon, Georgia	26
Augusta, Georgia	26
Columbia, South Carolina	26
Pittsburgh, Pennsylvania	27
Evansville, Indiana	27
Albuquerque, New Mexico	28
Los Angeles, California	28
Riverside, California	28
San Bernardino, California	28
San Diego, California	28
Salt Lake City, Utah	28–29
Wichita, Kansas	29
Philadelphia, Pennsylvania	29–30
Detroit, Michigan	30
Milwaukee, Wisconsin	30
Rockford, Illinois	30
Chicago, Illinois	30
Dover, Delaware	31
Wilmington, Delaware	31
Long Island, New York	31
New York City	31
Houston, Texas	November 2
Pasadena, Texas	2
Austin, Texas	2

Every stop had its special problems, of great moment at the time, mostly forgotten by now. It was exhausting just to make preparations in Washington for the proliferating stops. The strain on President Johnson had to be great. But with his amazing stamina and single-mindedness, he flew on, and on. Advance men were coming back to the office with a row of battle stars, colored metal tabs, clipped to their billfolds. The Secret Service agents distributed the changing insignia to persons authorized to be in restricted areas at each stop.

Thinking back, there was difficulty getting advance men into Wichita, Kansas—a late addition—on time. And advance men waited in vain at Madison, Wisconsin, which was scratched from the schedule. A touchy situation developed when somebody in the White House became sensitive about Goldwater signs and pickets appearing at LBJ rallies. Marvin Watson, by this time a special assistant to the president and emerging as a strong figure, called several of us over to the Fish Room in the White House and said that something had to be done about such irritations.

When I suggested ignoring them, the reply was, "What do you want to do, make policy in the field?"

We were told to pass along the word to advance men of the unhappiness caused by the pro-Goldwater activities at our rallies. I forgot or ignored the instruction until it was repeated, forcefully, a few days later. Thereafter I notified the advance men. An amusing incident followed. At one of the Southern stops, irritation provided by Goldwater zealots was minimal. The advance man was congratulated and asked what action had been taken. He had taken none, but on impulse he said that itching powder had been used on some of the Goldwaterites. His explanation may have been taken seriously, although he insists it was a joke.

Frequently it was necessary to keep our office open late into the night, and sometimes I went to a hotel for a few hours of sleep rather than go home. When the election was only days away, I checked into the nearby Roger Smith Hotel past midnight after closing the office. I went to sleep. The telephone rang. A White House operator had tracked me down. She asked me to hold for Bill Moyers, and his voice came on the line.

"John?"

"Yeah."

"Where are you?"

"I'm in the sack at the Roger Smith."

There was a pause. He chose to misunderstand me.

"John!" There was mock shock in his voice. "After all that's happened, you're in the sack with Roger Smith?"

That broke me up, 1 a.m. or 2 a.m., or whatever it was. The reason that he was calling was to suggest that I go down to Austin, Texas, for the elections and the expected celebration. I said that I was "beat, knocked out," that I planned to stay home and sleep through the elections. He and McCarthy were still at the White House, despite the late hour, and they were being thoughtful. Probably there would be a wing-ding of a celebration in Austin when the country had counted its ballots. I said okay, I would go.

I dispatched advance men up to the end. When the president went to Delaware, a squad of advance men went ahead of him. There was a feeling that he would be pleased, particularly if Republican Senator John J. Williams were defeated. It did not happen.

What did happen was that LBJ delivered one of those amazing country speeches filled with wise saws and instances at the Wilmington airport. I was not along, but one of the men who went told me about it. The part that got him was this:

> So you are going to have to select the man whose thumb will be close to that button. You are going to have to select the man who will answer that telephone, that "hot line" from Moscow, when the bell starts jingling, ting-a-ling-a-ling, and they say "Moscow is calling." You are going to have to select the president, and you have only one president.

It was the "ting-a-ling-a-ling" that was the special LBJ touch.

I went down to Austin for the big day. There was a surplus of manpower, so I did little. We met with Austin Congressman Jake Pickle, who was in charge of local arrangements, and we looked over motorcade routes and made arrangements for a platform at the head of Congress Street with the Texas state Capitol building in the background. McCarthy dealt with Governor Connally, and Hal Pachios handled the speech site. There was plenty of Texas help.

We stayed at the Driskill Hotel and partied in the Headliners Club there. While McCarthy was making arrangements with the hotel manager for the president's use of the hotel, he was offered the Jim Hogg suite for his own use. McCarthy suggested that I get my bags and move into the suite too because there were several rooms. This was the suite named after the Texas governor who had given his daughter the name of Ima, Ima Hogg. It was in Texas-range style, with longhorns and trophy heads on the walls and dark and heavy wooden trim and furnishings. As soon as we were settled, McCarthy hung up on a phone call and said, "We have to get out."

The president had decided to use the Hogg suite for a party for his old friends on election eve following his final speech in front of the Texas Capitol building. So we packed up again and got out from under the longhorns, returning to our rooms on the other side of the hotel.

In the large room, which we were using as our headquarters, telephone men installed telephones on a long table. We were to be in contact with Johnson headquarters around the country for fast election information. A less obvious purpose, I surmised, was to create activity that would justify the transportation of so many people from Washington. The telephone system was barely used.

Lyndon Johnson was on the way to Texas. He landed at Houston and spoke at three places: downtown, at Sam Houston High School, where he had once taught, and in front of a bank in suburban Pasadena. We heard that the crowds were as large as ever. Shortly after 8:30 p.m., he landed at Bergstrom Air Force Base and came to Austin. Police estimated that 75,000 people turned out to welcome him. With bullhorn in hand, standing in the motorcade, he invited the crowds lining the streets to "Come to the speakin'."

I did not go to the speakin', but returned to the hotel. The Secret Service agent in charge of the Jim Hogg suite for the party had asked me to help him identify the Johnsons' friends for admission to the suite. Although I suggested that he find someone better acquainted in Texas circles, he insisted, and I lent a hand. Later I wandered around to some of the other parties in progress in the hotel and then went to bed. The president and his family traveled to his ranch to spend the night.

The next day, Tuesday, November 3, Election Day, I was chagrined to see a news account of the arrest of six members of a United Steelworkers Union local in Houston on charges of aggravated assault.

They were accused of squirting oil of mustard and camphor on some high school boys who were passing out Goldwater literature in the crowd waiting for the president at Sam Houston High. When Marvin Watson came to the headquarters, I asked him if he had seen the newspapers. He had.

The president and Mrs. Johnson voted in Johnson City. In Austin, the public was invited to Municipal Auditorium that night to watch the election returns on a giant screen.

As the day waned, I used the elaborate and hardly touched telephone facilities in our headquarters once. When my trusty pocketwatch indicated that the polls were closed in the small towns of northern Maine, in Aroostook and Piscataquis counties, I called up the United Press International (UPI) bureau in Portland and asked for any returns from those towns, or "plantations," as some of them were called, in the old colonial sense of "planting" (settling) people rather than crops.

When I had operated Maine UPI bureaus, I had trained string correspondents in those areas to telephone in the earliest election returns as quickly as they were available. The practice had been continued. The returns given to me indicated clearly, if any doubt had been left, that Lyndon Johnson was a shoo-in. Not that there ever was much validity to the slogan, "As Maine goes, so goes the nation." In 1958, the last year of Maine's early election of state officials, I had researched Maine voting records from 1840 through 1956 and had found that in presidential years Maine had elected a governor in September of the same political persuasion as the president subsequently elected in November only 60 percent of the time, and from 1900 on, only 53 percent of the time. The distortion had begun with partisan enthusiasm aroused during the "Log Cabin and Hard Cider" campaign for the presidency in 1840. Edward Kent, a Whig, won the governorship of Maine. He led the Democratic nominee by a small margin in the popular voting in the early Maine election and was named governor after the close contest had been referred to the Maine legislature. The Whigs that year were trying to seat General William Henry Harrison in the White House, the military hero who had won the nickname "Tippecanoe" from his victory at Tippecanoe over Tecumseh's Indians. The Whigs saw a chance to capitalize on Kent's early victory and whipped up a chant that set the pattern for partisan appraisal of the Maine voting in years to come:

Oh, have you heard how old Maine went?
She went hell-bent for Governor Kent,
And Tippecanoe and Tyler, too.

A small plurality thus became a "hell-bent" victory. Political slogans, bah.

There remained one good weathervane in Maine voting, however. The small northern towns whose polls closed early traditionally went strongly Republican in presidential elections. Now, in 1964, the early returns showed these Republican strongholds crumbling. There was no hope for the aspirations of Barry Goldwater, so, Mr. Henry David Thoreau, rapid communications between Maine and Texas can be useful on occasion.

I did not bother with any more election returns. As a matter of fact, after dinner and a few conversations with people, I went up to my room. Washed out physically and emotionally, I lay awake and heard the noises of the hotel, hour by hour.

The next morning I learned of President Johnson's victory statement that had been made in the early hours of the day. He had spoken in the Municipal Auditorium, where he had gone with his family when everyone but Senator Goldwater had "called" the election. There was to be barbecue at the ranch. I caught a plane for Washington.

In succeeding days I took my belongings from the desk at Democratic National Committee headquarters and signed on again in my old job. A thank-you note came, signed by Jack Valenti. And on November 13, this wire arrived from the White House:

YOU ARE CORDIALLY INVITED TO A COFFEE AND THANK YOU FELLOWSHIP FROM 6:30 TO 7:30 P.M. WEDNESDAY, NOVEMBER 18, IN THE WHITE HOUSE STAFF MESS. PLEASE PRESENT THIS WIRE AT THE SOUTHWEST GATE. RSVP BY CALLING MARY WHITE OR NELL YATES IN MY OFFICE.

JACK VALENTI, SPECIAL ASSISTANT
TO THE PRESIDENT

My secretary pencilled on it "You have accepted," and in ink after "COFFEE" the words "and water" were inserted subsequently in my handwriting.

Advance men who had preceded the president throughout the country gathered convivially in the White House mess. I had imagined that "COFFEE" was a euphemism. But there it was, brown and hot. For those who did not drink coffee, there were tall glasses of ice and water. I remembered my college days when a coed who sometimes organized beer parties sent out invitations to a tea. We laughed and found it unfunny when she served tea.

For each guest there was a ninety-five-cent paperback copy of *My Hope for America* by Lyndon B. Johnson (New York: Random House, 1964).

"Hey!" said one of the harbingers. "There's nothing written on mine."

A secretary attending the party took his book into another room and added the inscription.

The president came downstairs, thanked us for our activities, and went back upstairs.

The advance men stood with their coffee cups and glasses of ice water and looked at one another.

"We will hold our own party," said Wilson McCarthy.

We hired the back room of Duke Ziebert's restaurant and put on a black-tie dinner. Since there was no other way to pay for it, each honored guest paid $15. The advance men came, the presidential assistants came, but the president did not. Skilled at limiting the seating at head tables, we restricted this one to three people: McCarthy, Byrne, and Bruno. Underwood and McCarthy had had a falling out, and Marty did not come.

Instead of formal speeches, there were presentations of numerous useful awards, such as a suit of toy Italian armor for a Secret Service agent who had been manhandled by a crowd. Moyers, I recall, received a film director's megaphone, Valenti a kewpie doll with a hinged jaw and the words "Where's Wilson?" on the plastic base. My award, in honor of a notorious $3.19 pocketwatch, was an illuminated Budweiser clock from a barroom wall. Pat Kennedy received the "First Marvin Watson Award for the most Goldwater signs at any campaign rally." That was in Milwaukee at an LBJ visit he advanced.

The 1964 campaign ended there at Duke Zeibert's restaurant. Ahead were a remarkable record of presidential achievement in domestic legislation, the deepening morass of Southeast Asia, and the imperious dismantling of the apparatus of a major political party.

An Advance Man's Contemplation and Photographs

JFK gave his last talks on a gray day in November
in Fort Worth, Texas "where the West begins."
The town grown from a post of frontier soldiers,
and trailhead for the drives of cattle drovers
became an aircraft builder for national defense.
The warmth of reception it gave JFK this day
heartened his campaign as it got underway.

President Kennedy speaks to an outdoor audience in Fort Worth on November 22, 1963 before addressing chamber of commerce meeting. *Fort Worth Star-Telegram Collection, Special Collection, the University of Texas at Arlington Library, Arlington, Texas.*

The advance man surveyed
arrangements for departure.
Dallas was next on the itinerary.

The morning scene in Fort Worth before formation of the motorcade for departure. Advance man with folded arms under hotel marquee keeps an eye on preparations. *The Fort Worth Star-Telegram.*

Caught by the camera on this fateful day,
John F. Kennedy is standing tall
in the forming Fort Worth motorcade.
He's full of life, impatient to be off.

You sense the vigor and the charm and steel
that made him president and brought him here
to reconfirm the role he'd won before.
Thus far he's savored warmth from common folk
who've lined the streets—and will again today.
But conflict is the journalistic style
and here it dwells upon a party split
between the Texas governor's elite
and the senator inclined toward working folk.

Look elsewhere in the frame and you can see
some "business" going on, like sly asides
in paintings that the elder Brueghel made:
an advance man joining with a White House aide
to seat the senator and LBJ,
mentor of the Texas governor,
together in the idling motorcade.
They try to harmonize the dissonance
beloved of the watching journalists.

The Fort Worth motorcade forms with special seating arrangements. While JFK enters his car (lower right), the advance man shows LBJ to his seat (upper left) in the vice presidential car as Secret Service agent Rufus W. Youngblood helps LBJ with his coat. *The Fort Worth Star-Telegram.*

The line of cars has formed and rolls through town,
pausing for a joyous welcoming
from shining faces always to be young.

Then there's a flight and second motorcade—
and suddenly a vibrant life is gone.
Euphoria explodes in horrid grief
that rockets 'round the earth.

A crowd of school children on the motorcade route awaits the Kennedys. *Fort Worth Star-Telegram Collection, Special Collections, the University of Texas at Arlington Library, Arlington, Texas.*

Grief stays on for promise unfulfilled,
as well as for the human life destroyed
by bullets in a fit of crazy hate.
But there's a kind of politics to lead
and someone else must take the victim's place.
There's Lyndon Johnson in another frame,
beginning his campaign on Labor Day
in Labor's premier city of Detroit.
A harbinger there puts names to faces,
then oversees the speakin' places.

President and Mrs. Johnson arrive in Detroit for the formal opening of the presidential campaign on September 7, 1964. Advance man makes introductions. *LBJ Library.*

A sitting president by default,
a candidate, then nominee,
Johnson sounded like all three
speaking simultaneously.
But one thing about campaigning
in the Lyndon Johnson style.
He loved to shake the hand
of every person he could reach.
Bruised and buffeted he'd come back
from many an airport fence,
bleeding scratches on his hands,
a smile upon his face.

At the General Dynamics submarine plant in Groton, Connecticut on June 3, 1964, LBJ shakes many hands. *LBJ Library.*

He left the innovation
to the faithful Lady Bird
who roamed the South by whistlestop
where he was seldom heard.

Lady Bird Johnson campaigns for her husband in a whistlestop tour through the South in October 1964. *LBJ Library.*

New England was a bonanza
for Lyndon Johnson's cause
and JFK's remembrance,
that vibrant life cut short.

LBJ begins his September 28, 1964 marathon New England campaign trip here in Providence, Rhode Island, and visits all states in the region before returning to Washington, D.C. *LBJ Library.*

But San Francisco topped them all
for turning out the crowds.
The newspapers reported
half a million gathered
for his visit there in June,
One compared the numbers
to the throngs of V-J Day.

Huge crowds turn out to greet LBJ along San Francisco's Market Street on June 19, 1964. *LBJ Library.*

LBJ, delighted,
vowed a second visit
before election day.

President Johnson returns to San Francisco for its Columbus Day celebration on October 11, 1964. That's California Governor Pat Brown to the President's right, the advance man to the president's left. *Gene Wright, photographer.*

The candidate was winding up
as the fall campaign wound down.
Johnson campaigned with a fierce concentration
in cities and towns throughout the nation,
ending in Texas on the eve of election.
He took to the streets like an ancient Town Crier
with modernized bullhorn and motorcade driver,
all the while shouting "Come to the speakin',"
his Hill Country name for "political teach-in."
Framed by the curve of the statehouse dome,
he thanked the crowd gathered to welcome him home.
He said he had tried to fulfill expectations
of John Kennedy for whom he stood in his stead,
and he hoped tens of millions would be on their side.
They were, on the morrow, in a massive landslide
which he took as a mandate to produce legislation,
and that's what he did in rapid succession.
The best of it all made equality law.

President Johnson campaigns with his trademark hat flailing in Cleveland on October 8, 1964. *LBJ Library.*

But praise for extending the reach of the law
to prevent racial exclusions
was soon overcome by the misguided war
which our country had become engaged in.
LBJ and his cadre of president's men
would not withdraw from the civil war
into which we should not have intruded.

President Johnson addressing a crowd in Indianapolis on July 24, 1964. A larger banner supports his continuing war policy. *LBJ Library.*

But the toll of that war caused him to withdraw
from seeking to win reelection.
Though the Vietnam War is a blot on his past,
LBJ's list of what he did best
is a long litany of legislation.
Progressive in nature and wide in its scope
it opened new channels for conveying hope
to the poorest parts of the nation.

War protesters cross the Memorial Bridge in Washington, D.C. during the March on the Pentagon on October 21, 1967. *LBJ Library.*

His term expired, candidacy undone,
Johnson retired to the ranch he would run
instead of a nation and voice in the world.
When he died he was buried in the land that he loved,
the Texas Hill Country by the Pedernales River.

Lyndon Baines Johnson returns to his ranch near Stonewall, Texas at the conclusion of his presidency. *LBJ Library.*

JFK lies under a flickering flame
on a hillock which overlooks Washington.
Here among others who served their country
is the young president slain in his prime,
deprived of his role as a leader of men,
lost to the promise of what lay ahead,
no longer to savor the salt taste of ocean
wafted in breezes of the Cape's summertime.

This portrait photograph of John Fitzgerald Kennedy was distributed by the White House during his presidency. *JFK Library.*

Assassination melded two presidencies,
although old loyalties caused some unease.
The split was surmounted in campaign '64,
another came later on the Vietnam War.
Should we still try to win or should we withdraw?
LBJ chose engagement, to battle and stay.
Opponents erupted in angry dismay.
Nobody knows what JFK would have done
had he survived Dallas on that fateful day.
Contention took over. Nobody won,
at least in the party of Jefferson.
The landslide consensus of year '64,
by year '68 had been argued away.

War, racial troubles, elections,
legislation, a mail order gun, more
assassinations, Robert Kennedy,
Martin Luther King—all jumbled together
in the 'Sixties decade
as its tumultuous history was made,
some of it good, some of it bad,
some of it terribly, terribly sad.

The author, second from left, introduces young Mayor Robert Couturier of Lewiston, Maine to President and Mrs. Johnson on August 20, 1967. Senator Edmund Muskie of Maine is to the President's left. *Lewiston Sun-Journal.*

CHAPTER 9

The Rocky, Nonpartisan
Coast of Maine

I drifted away from advance work after the 1964 elections, became, you might say, a harbinger emeritus. One or two calls from the White House came at awkward times for my regular job, and I made excuses. There was no pressure. The campaign was over. Life was back to normal. Wilson McCarthy had gone to work for Hollywood movie studios. Only twice more did I go out in front of President Johnson. The last advance was in 1966, and it took me back to Maine, where my brush with politics had begun. But before that, in 1965, there was one quick trip to the Midwest, sandwiched between the 1964 campaign and that final advance to Maine. The Midwest trip began on short notice, was over quickly, and was notable chiefly for that *bete noire* of the advance man: motorcade trouble. Floods and tornadoes had struck the Midwest in the spring of 1965, and President Johnson decided to look at the disaster of the affected states. Bill Moyers telephoned at dinnertime and asked if I could fly to Minneapolis-St. Paul almost immediately to set the stage for the president's visit there the following day to view flood damage caused by the Mississippi River. I agreed and went to the White House for a quick briefing, which also was attended by Marty Underwood, who was bound for Toledo, Ohio, on a similar mission and Jerry Bruno, who was headed for South Bend, Indiana. Tornadoes had occurred in seven states, and floods had inundated parts of Minnesota. The president would inspect the damage from the ground at the three places where we were going and would fly over other sections of the disaster area. Buford Ellington, director of the Office of Emergency Planning, who was in charge of federal assistance for the stricken states, would accompany the president and the elected officials.

We were airborne soon after the briefing ended and arrived at our destinations in the middle of the night. With Minnesota state and local officials I toured the riverfront, despite the hour, and chose the place from which LBJ would view the floodwaters. It was at the edge of the surging Mississippi in St. Paul. There a plant of the Northern States Power Company, which ordinarily could be reached on foot, was surrounded by rushing waters. Workmen in slickers and lifebelts labored under floodlights, packing sandbags around the isolated plant and along the road upon which we stood. Small boats carried the workmen between the plant and what, if it had not been raining, could have been considered dry land. Pump hoses snaked over piles of sandbags. Motors throbbed. Debris hurtled downstream. Photographers here could catch the sweeping floodwaters and the efforts of men to achieve control.

The president was in Minneapolis-St. Paul only fifty minutes at midday, but that was enough for things to go wrong. The viewing site was effective for news coverage, although it was touch-and-go, finally go, whether local safety officials would permit the motorcade to reach the chosen site because of the threat of rising waters. There was a respectable crowd at the airport, despite the preoccupations of the people of the flood-beset area. But the motorcade had been botched. Secret Service agents had encountered difficulty in obtaining a suitable limousine for the president's use on short notice and had settled for a car with fewer seats. Incredibly, I had ignored this development. When Air Force One arrived, local congressmen had to scramble for seats in the motorcade, wondering out loud why they had been summoned to accompany the president if they were not to ride with him in their own backyard. Then the hasty liaison with local police proved faulty. Public buses and private cars pushed into the motorcade at intersections on the way to the viewing site because of the lack of proper traffic control. The police, of course, had other concerns because of the flood emergency. But I was more pleased than usual to see Air Force One back in the air.

The day, however, did not improve.

Mac Kilduff, assistant White House press secretary, and I were talking on the airport apron while the news correspondents were filing their stories. I was needling Kilduff about his practice of surreptitiously switching the identification signs between VIP and press buses just before motorcades loaded in order to put newsmen in front of the brass, a practice that I secretly applauded. Kilduff tapped my shoulder.

"Isn't that your plane taking off?"

A Jetstar was whistling down the runway. I was supposed to have charge of a Jetstar to take crews from the Minnesota and Indiana stops back to Washington.

"No," I said, "our ship is on the other side of the hangar over there. The pilot is waiting for me to give the word."

"I think that was yours," said Kilduff. "You'd better come back on the press plane."

I was sure of myself. The reporters straggled back to the press plane, and it took off. I went looking for our Jetstar. Kilduff had been right. One of the president's military aides had swiped it.

After a tedious wait, those of us stranded rode back to Washington in an old Constellation, which was carrying communications men and hauling audio equipment from the Midwest stops. We could have returned faster in a blimp.

The president barely had touched down on the 1965 visit to Minnesota's Twin Cities. The advance there had taken a few hours. Nearly a week would be spent on the more complex preparations for LBJ's August 20, 1966, visit to Maine, the last leg on his journey to Campobello Island, New Brunswick. On that Canadian island lying off of Maine's eastern extremity, Johnson and Prime Minister Lester Pearson of Canada were to dedicate a visitors' pavilion under construction in front of the red-shingled summer home that had belonged to Franklin D. Roosevelt. But LBJ would not travel as the crow flies to perform that ceremonial duty. He would go to Campobello by way of upper New York State, by way of Rhode Island and New Hampshire and Vermont and Maine. He would see a few people.

I was minding the business of my regular job when Marty Underwood and Hal Pachios telephoned from the White House, although Underwood was still based at the Department of Commerce. He was making a career of advance work, and Pachios served on the staff of Bill Moyers, who had become press secretary. They had returned from a trip survey to New England, still concerned over where the president would stay overnight. The aging Roosevelt house on Campobello, they said, was unsuitable for the president and his entourage, and they had explored Maine's eastern coast without discovering a good alternative. They had been talking over the problems with Marvin Watson, who was now head monitor at the White House, and it was decided that they should ask me to continue the search and to handle the Maine part of the advance.

"Sure," I said, always willing to go to Maine and more willing than ever in August.

About the overnight arrangements, one of them said, Bar Harbor might be the best bet, even though it was not far enough down east to be close to Campobello. Bowdoin College owned the old Oakes mansion at Bar Harbor, which was a possibility. But the urgent thing was to get to Maine quickly.

"Hey!" I said, "I wrote that script. Let me get a bag."

Pachios said that the Secret Service agent in charge of the Maine security arrangements would meet me on a late-day commercial flight to Boston. We would switch to a Bangor flight and be met by a car for the forty-six-mile run into Bar Harbor.

"Who's the agent?"

"Bill Livingood."

"What's he look like?

"Light, curly hair."

"Okay, I'll meet him on the 5 o'clock plane."

On the plane in the seat behind me was a young man on the short side with light curly hair. But that kind of hair on males flying to New England that afternoon was not unusual. A voice behind me asked a stewardess if she could page someone for him. She demurred. I turned in my seat and saw the familiar Secret Service identification being held out to the reluctant stewardess.

"Never mind, Bill," I said. "Move over."

As we exchanged skimpy information on the way to Bangor about the forthcoming presidential trip, I said, "What did they tell you I looked like?"

"They said to look for a short cigaret stub in the corner of a mouth, and that you would be the guy behind it."

The light hair and the cigaret stub spent the next couple of days chasing what proved to be a will-o'-the-wisp in the Bar Harbor area: a presidential lodging for the night. Not that good possibilities were lacking. Harold (Tubby) Collier, an influential Republican businessman who was set on a president of the United States visiting Bar Harbor, was our guide, and a good one. The Oakes mansion, known as the Oakes Center, where conferences were held, was spacious, although the space was chopped up for current usage. It was also a bit seedy for the taste of some. Another major drawback was its location next to the pier of the Bar Harbor-Yarmouth (Nova Scotia) ferry. In my mind's ear I could hear the ferry horn hooting and rousing the president from his sleep. The kitchen was antique but adequate. The White House would bring in its own cooks and equipment. All the center would have to provide would be someone who knew the house. The couple who ran it for Bowdoin College was available.

While we were considering the problem of overnight accommodations, we drove to Acadia National Park, and with Superintendent Tom Hyde we looked over the Acadia Job Corps Conservation Center, which had opened the previous April. There were 124 boys in the camp receiving instruction in basic forestry and construction skills. An inspection of the new camp by the president would provide another reason for stopping in the Bar Harbor area.

I talked over the possibilities with Collier. Air Force One could land at Dow Air Force Base in Bangor, and the presidential party, plus a press pool, could helicopter to Bar Harbor and land on the baseball field. The president and Mrs. Johnson could settle into the house at about 5–6 p.m. while the press buses came down from Bangor. Then there could be an inspection of the Job Corps camp, followed by some event on the Village Green to give the New England flavor. The meal could be served in the house any time the Johnsons wanted it. The next day, Sunday, the party could helicopter to Campobello for the international ceremony. It would be a boring bus trip for the reporters over those interminable blueberry barrens of eastern Maine, and they would have to be ready to leave at dawn. But there was no help for that.

I gave my initial report to the White House, to someone new to me, Sherman Markman. I included the reservations about the Oakes house. We would continue looking, I told him. Livingood was in touch with his people, and the Oakes mansion was adequate from the Secret Service standpoint. After driving us all over the Bar Harbor area, Collier put us up for the night in his own house.

There were various offers for other houses the next day.

The most promising was of "Sea Change," the modern home of former ambassador to Belgium, William A. M. Burden, at Northeast Harbor near Sargent Head. We drove there, noting that it was twelve miles from Bar Harbor and took about twenty minutes. The Burdens showed us through the house and the cottages as well as a grandiose air raid shelter built into a knoll. The living room, paneled in knotty gray wood (was it Spanish cypress?), looked out on Frenchman's Bay and the ocean. The former ambassador and I walked along the shore and talked about Washington, where he had seen considerable federal service, including a term as assistant secretary of commerce. I asked him what his current occupation was, and he said that he kept an office in New York, where he "managed the family investments."

Inside, Mrs. Burden said that if the presidential party was to come to her home she must know as soon as possible how many she should expect to dinner. I hedged rather than described the customary procedure because, after all, we were just looking. I did not think it necessary at that point to mention that when the offer of a house was accepted, the White House expected to assume control. The president has too many responsibilities to be in the position of a guest.

Congratulating the Burdens on their beautiful home and thanking them for inviting the president to stay there, I said that I would be back in touch with them. As it turned out, however, we could not accept their offer because someone in the White House had come to the conclusion while we were inspecting the Burdens' home that the president should speak in Lewiston, Maine, rather than Bar Harbor. No one told me why, and like that fellow who carried the word to Garcia, I did not ask. There were obvious considerations. The mid-term congressional elections were less than three months away, and Lewiston, a textile city with a dominant population of Franco-Americans, was staunchly Democratic. Bar Harbor usually voted Republican. The physical problems of transporting the temporary White House to the resort on Mt. Desert Island, where Bar Harbor is situated, also were serious.

When I returned to Collier's home, the change in plans came to me via another new voice from the White House, Jim Jones, a Watson assistant. The Secret Service agent and I were to abandon our efforts in Bar Harbor and go to Brunswick, the home of Bowdoin College, where Nathaniel Hawthorne and Henry Wadsworth Longfellow went to school. That coastal community, more pertinently, is also the home of the Brunswick Naval Air Station, where the presidential plane would land according to the new scheme. I was to be sent assistance for the advance because there would be three stops in Maine on Saturday, August 20. Not only would there be the landing at Brunswick and the speech at Lewiston, but the presidential party would be boarding the *USS Northampton* at Portland afterwards. The cruiser, a seaborne command ship for the Atlantic fleet, would take the presidential party to Campobello and, very neatly, solve the problem of overnight accommodations.

Tubby Collier, understandably, was disappointed when I told him that Bar Harbor would not be on the itinerary. He refused to give up, however, and succeeded in getting the press buses routed to Bar Harbor on their way to Campobello. The visiting reporters stayed overnight and were treated to a sumptuous clambake, even though they were hours late arriving in Bar Harbor.

We drove west to Brunswick and put our bags in the Siesta Motel. While the Secret Service agent went to the Navy field, I telephoned George Mitchell, a Portland lawyer and former member of Senator Muskie's staff, who later would be majority leader of the U.S. Senate and an international troubleshooter. Mitchell, an old friend, was one of the White House's designated contacts in Maine. He was then Democratic state chairman. Mitchell drove to the Siesta and from there phoned Lewiston Mayor Robert L. Couturier and asked him to come over and "meet the White House representative."

"I visited the president in Washington at the National Conference of Mayors," Couturier said with a smile when he arrived. "Now he is returning my visit."

A former radio announcer serving his second term as mayor but still in his early twenties, Couturier, I gathered, could be sensitive about his official prerogatives. I made a point of asking whom I should deal with at City Hall during his absence. He had said that he was going to Canada for a few days but would be back in time to greet the president. We talked over the format for the visit to Lewiston.

The next day some plainclothesmen from the Maine State Police came to the motel to go over plans for the president's protection. I dropped by Livingood's room to meet them and found myself shaking hands with Detective Sergeant Millard Nickerson, whom I had not seen since I left Augusta in 1961.

"How's your imposter?" I asked him.

He grinned. "Haven't seen him lately."

Nickerson and another State Police detective had gone out from Rockland in a Coast Guard cutter on a squally winter's day in 1956, Valentine's Day, February 14, to the island of North Haven to arrest Ferdinand Waldo Demara Jr., the imposter to end all imposters. Under another man's name, and credentials, Demara was playing schoolteacher in the island school. They took him to Augusta.

I was running behind the AP on the breaking story by the time I got to see Nickerson. I pressed him again and again about how they had confirmed that the big, red-faced island schoolteacher was Demara.

"Did you have fingerprints? Did somebody bring something in with his prints on it?"

"Well, yeah. But why not lay off now? It's bad enough."

When you have been a reporter long enough, you can shorten up the game of Twenty Questions.

"Let's see, it probably was a container. Was it a beer can?"

"Come on. Don't make it any worse."

"Was it a beer can?"

"Yeah."

It made a good lead, if you like those things. You have to when you are in the wire services.

I talked to Demara in the Kennebec County attorney's office. I came in from the windy street wearing my trenchcoat and a tweed cap.

"Well-l-l," he said, looking at coat and cap, "where did you park your M.G.?"

The county attorney was soft on him. Demara never seemed to hurt anyone but himself, but I have always wondered about the surgery he did on those Korean War casualties while playing Dr. Joseph Cyr, surgeon lieutenant on the destroyer Cayuga of the Canadian Navy. If you can believe the stories, the surgery came out all right. But how have his patients weathered the years?

The court let him go with his promise to go home to Lawrence, Massachusetts, and to go straight. He was contrite. He would put his great talents to honest employment. He boarded the bus for Boston. A book about him says he went home. He did, eventually. But first he got off in Portland.

Ferdinand Demara, player of many roles. Faces from the past set me off.

The next day we drove around the triangle, Brunswick to Lewiston to Portland to Brunswick. We decided where the president's plane would be parked and where the crowd would assemble at Brunswick Naval Air Station. We looked over John F. Kennedy Memorial Park in Lewiston, where Johnson would make his address. We went through the Maine State Pier on Portland's waterfront, where he would board the Northampton. We inspected possible motorcade routes and helicopter landing sites. Jones had indicated that there would be helicopters to take the party from Brunswick to Lewiston and then to Portland. In Lewiston there were several possible sites for landing the helicopters. In Portland, the ball field or parking lot of Jack Junior High School, about one and a half miles from the pier, looked like the closest landing area.

Back in Brunswick we met a plane from Washington that brought us some assistance. In addition to more Secret Service agents and specialists from the White House Communications Agency, there were two men to help with the advances: Albert Gamache, administrative assistant to Congressman William D. Hathaway of Lewiston, and a former Texas schoolteacher by the name of Douglas Nobles, who was part of the new Southwest look at the White House. Gamache knew all of the Lewiston public officials, which would be a help, and Nobles appeared agreeable and willing.

We decided to make our headquarters the Flamingo Motel in Lewiston, because the major activity would be in that city. The White House switchboard would be installed there. When the move was made from Brunswick, the detailed work of organizing three separate Maine stops began. Shepard (Shep) Lee, an old acquaintance who owned an automobile dealership in Lewiston-Auburn, assisted by providing cars to Nobles and me so that we could work on different stops. I introduced Nobles to people with whom he would be working in Portland and set him to making the arrangements for a send-off for the Johnsons at the foot of the Maine State Pier, freeing myself to concentrate on the Brunswick and Lewiston stops. Gamache was working principally for his congressman, who would be master of ceremonies for the speaking program in Lewiston.

For a time after the Lewiston location for the president's visit had been decided upon, the White House sought an excuse for the president's forthcoming presence in Lewiston. A visit to the Maine State Products Show there was considered and discarded as less than thrilling. A proposed Democratic picnic was rejected as not being in keeping with the tenor of the president's tour. An inspection of the Job Corps Center for Women at nearby Poland Spring was looked upon with favor, but only for a time. I reconnoitered the center that had been established in the old wooden buildings of the Poland Spring House, one of Maine's famous resorts that had succumbed to the Age of Tourism.

The man in charge of security at the center turned out to be Robert Marx, who was chief of the Maine State Police when I was in the State

House. After years of directing law enforcement activities throughout the state of Maine, Marx, who had retired from the State Police, found himself supervising "date night" each weekend. While I was speaking with Sol Ernst, director of the center, there was a telephone call for me from Washington. The Poland Spring visit was rubbed out before I had sketched it in. The president would make a substantive speech in Lewiston, and there was no need to scout up other activities, I was told. On the return to Lewiston, four miles away, I meditated out loud about people who could not make up their minds. This new White House bunch was jumpy. Ah well, before I had left Poland Spring I had arranged for a contingent of the girls in their blazers to be bused to Kennedy Park to swell the crowd for the president's speech.

There was, however, a greater difficulty in making arrangements on this occasion than the skipping about from place to place. It lay in the peculiar consensus politics that the president appeared to be playing. With an eye on the approaching congressional elections, was LBJ embarking on a campaign trip? Principal Republican as well as Democratic officeholders were to be in his entourage all along the route. The White House was repeatedly using the term *nonpolitical* to describe the trip. What, then, had the president in mind in swinging through five states on his way to Canada at this particular time, a bipartisan cluster of political luminaries around him? Was he playing Big Daddy, the President of All the People? Or was he Reynard the Fox, using the Republicans against themselves?

On an advance there never was much time to ponder the niceties of intention. But on this one the presidential ambivalence was causing a serious practical problem. Certainly Senator Edmund S. Muskie, Maine's premier Democrat, would be along. And Democratic Congressman Bill Hathaway would be the master of ceremonies at the speakin' in Lewiston. But Senator Margaret Chase Smith, Governor John H. Reed, and Congressman Stanley R. Tupper, all Republicans, would be in the official party to reap whatever benefits that public exposure with the president might provide.

Muskie's Senate seat was not at stake in the 1966 elections. But Margaret Chase Smith and Governor Reed were candidates. Tupper was not seeking reelection. Under the ground rules communicated to me by Markman and confirmed by Jones, the Democratic opponents of Senator Smith and Governor Reed and the Democratic candidate for Congress in Maine's first district could not take an active part in the president's visit. State Senator Elmer H. Violette, who was opposing

Mrs. Smith, Secretary of State Kenneth M. Curtis, who was challenging Reed, and Portland attorney Peter N. Kyros, who was contesting a former Republican congressman's attempt at a comeback, would be excluded from the official party, motorcades, and the platform at Lewiston. Some Maine Democrats said publicly that if this was the kind of campaign assistance proffered by Lyndon Johnson, he could help best by shooting deer at his ranch. In the volatile Lewiston City Democratic Committee, member Joseph T. Poulin proposed a boycott of the Lewiston appearance and said that he was "goin' fishin'."

It was in this atmosphere that we proceeded to make preparations. I repeatedly told Markman of the dismay and anger of Maine Democrats that threatened to make a shambles of the visit. But no changes were permitted in the format. So in Portland I made sure to include the chairman of the Portland and South Portland city councils and the Portland city manager on the reception committees. In Lewiston the mayors of Lewiston and Auburn and the chairman of the Board of County Commissioners were among those invited to greet the president. And at Brunswick the chairman of the board of selectmen was asked to join the reception line, as were the two ranking Navy captains at the air station. Wives, of course, were included. We obeyed all the rules of the nonpartisan game.

At Lewiston, the city agreed to redecorate the drab, octagonal bandstand, string new electric lines to it, and build a jutting platform for the speakers. The public works department began to construct the platform on the traditional side facing City Hall, but I had the workmen move it ninety degrees so that it faced the short end of the park. Kennedy Park in Lewiston is a large one for a small city. If enough Democrats became angry, it might be hard to pack in a crowd on a Saturday afternoon in August. I also gave the workmen specifications for a platform for television and still picture cameramen, this to be built, at a forty-five degree angle, of course, off to the left of the podium. And I asked the city to provide tables for the writing press. Yellow press passes and white Official passes—it was to come out "offical" unfortunately—were ordered from a Lewiston printer. *The Lewiston Sun and Journal* agreed to accredit the regional and local press. Young Democrats turned out hokey signs, and the Montagnard Club band practiced "Hail to the Chief." Now all we needed were people.

At Portland, the site was a difficult one. You came off Commercial Street on the waterfront with its bumpy railroad tracks to the narrow entrance to the Maine State Pier, where the *Northampton* was to be berthed. We could squeeze in a band and a VIP section, but the crowd would have to spill down the sides of the pier sheds. An ugly building, the Galt Block, formed an unfortunate backdrop. It resembled the Texas Book Depository in Dallas.

Brunswick would be a simple airport stop. There would be the official greeting, some handshaking along the fence, and the departure by motorcade. For motorcade it was to be. The helicopter plan had been dropped. A large press contingent would be traveling with the president, and, if all the reporters were to have the opportunity to cover his speech at Lewiston, a motorcade, including press buses, would be necessary. The drive from Brunswick to Lewiston is about thirty-five minutes, from Lewiston to Portland about forty-five minutes. We laid out the route.

On Friday, August 19, 1966, the day before president Johnson's visit to Maine, Senator Muskie was engaged in the Senate in protecting the Administration's Demonstration Cities (later Model Cities) bill from an attack mounted by Republican Senator John G. Tower of Texas. Muskie was the bill's floor manager. News reports were to credit his arguments on behalf of the measure, which was designed to rebuild and restore decaying neighborhoods in cities, with rallying broad support, including some previously reluctant Southerners. The vote was 53 to 22 in favor of the legislation. Afterward, Muskie caught a plane to Maine. En route by car to his home at China Lake near Waterville, Muskie stopped for dinner at a steak house close to the Flamingo, and I went to talk with him by previous arrangement. George Mitchell and Richard McMahon, another Muskie associate of long standing, were with him.

Senator Muskie was angry. When he had disembarked from the plane in Portland he was handed a copy of the *Portland Evening Express*. The headline on the lead story was: GOP MAY GET BIGGEST DIVIDEND FROM PRESIDENT'S VISIT TO MAINE. He showed me the newspaper story. It went on to say that although President Johnson's trip was being billed as nonpolitical, some Maine Democrats "were grousing because it appeared that Republican candidates may be getting the bulk of whatever benefits come from being in the limelight with the president." Muskie was not only incensed about the effect of the presidential visit on the Maine Democratic Party, which he had nurtured, but he also found irony in the fact that he had been serving as the administration's spokesman in the Senate at a time when preparations were being made for the visit to Maine under such insensitive guidelines.

I told him of my instructions and my repeated calls to the White House to question them.

"Is there anybody here in Maine I should talk to?" he asked.

"No," I said, "I'm it here. But Marvin Watson is your man. If you want to come over to the motel when you are through eating, I'll get our switchboard to track him down."

Muskie agreed.

I left for the motel, and, back in my room, I picked up a phone and asked the communications man on the switchboard to find out where Marvin Watson was. The phone rang back. Watson was en route to Ellenville, New York, in the Catskills, where the president was to spend the night.

When Senator Muskie came into my motel room, Air Force One was landing at Stewart Air Force Base at West Point, New York. The operator could not contact the plane. Then Watson was in the motorcade. Our switchboard man kept an open line to the "Catskills White House," the hotel in Ellenville. The motorcade lasted for a long time. Tired and irritated, Senator Muskie rose and said that he could not wait any longer. He added that he might not attend the Maine events the next day, that he might go directly to Campobello Island for the Sunday ceremony.

The switchboard operator suddenly had Watson on the line.

Watson had entered the hotel lobby in Ellenville.

"Hold on for Senator Muskie in Maine," I told Watson.

Muskie took the telephone and, after the usual greetings, said, "I want to read you the afternoon paper."

He read the headline and a few paragraphs of the newspaper story to Watson and then told him in straightforward terms what effect the supposedly nonpartisan visit was having on Maine politically.

Watson apparently asked the senator what remedial action could be taken. Muskie told him: the Democratic candidates, Violette, Curtis, and Kyros, should be in the receiving line at Brunswick and on the platform at Lewiston; they should travel with the motorcade in Maine; Violette and Curtis should be on the cruise to Campobello on the *Northampton*, since their opponents would be guests on the ship; Republican officeholders should be treated formally: and Maine legislative leaders, Democrats that year, should be included in the receiving line at Brunswick to greet the president as he entered Maine.

Watson did not balk at any of it.

The senator left for China Lake, and Mitchell began to contact the candidates to give them the news. Jim Jones called from Ellenville on the other line with a list of things I should do. I told him that I had a fair idea of what they were and ticked them off for him.

Violette lived in Aroostook County, far to the north, and would have to fly down. I telephoned Captain David C. Rains, commanding officer of the naval station at Brunswick, and obtained permission for a light plane of a north country flying service to land at the military field the next day. Then I figured out the seating for the motorcade and checked it out with the Secret Service agents. And then I went to bed.

We had most of the day Saturday to make certain that arrangements that were supposed to have been made actually had been made. I drove around the triangle, checking. Back at Brunswick the navy agreed to transport directly to Portland the luggage of all who were to travel to Campobello on the cruiser, relieving me of a bothersome detail.

Senator and Mrs. Muskie arrived at Brunswick early. The tension of the night before was gone. Air Force One was due to land at 4:25 p.m. but was a trifle over an hour late coming in from Burlington, Vermont. From the plane about fifteen minutes out of Brunswick, Jim Jones rang me at Base Operations. We checked last-minute signals, including car assignments. I told him that I had added an extra VIP car at the tail for Violette, Curtis, and Kyros rather than put them on the guest bus. Part of the game is not to confront the White House with surprises. There was a pause, as though Jones were talking over this development with someone. He came back on. "You had better put them in the bus."

There were about 5,000 people at the airfield when the plane touched down. With the greetings and handshakings over and the motorcade ready to move, I ran for the lead car so that I would be out in front to introduce the receiving line to the president at Kennedy Park in Lewiston. When the motorcade had passed over the bridge spanning the Androscoggin River from Brunswick to Topsham, the presidential limousine stopped at a frozen custard stand, which displayed a sign reading "Dairy Queen Welcomes LBJ." Looking back, I saw an agent buy some cones. He handed one of them to the president. The motorcade started up again and resumed speed.

The road between Brunswick and Lewiston did not lead through a Brooklyn or a San Francisco. Rural folk stood in clusters here and there. Sizable crowds lined the road in the towns of Lisbon and Lisbon Falls and along the Lewiston approach streets. A good crowd was packed in front of the bandstand in Kennedy Park. Police estimated its size, following a suggestion, at 25,000. Inflated numbers, unfortunately, are a way of life in the world of the advance man. A good crowd has to be made better.

Lewiston's young mayor was at the head of the receiving line, and I introduced him to the president and Mrs. Johnson. Then, keeping several feet behind the line to stay out of photographs, I introduced the others to Mr. Johnson and his wife. While there was milling around the bandstand, Couturier told me that the president had remembered meeting "the youngest mayor in the country" at the Conference of Mayors. The youthful face of the mayor as he wandered among the dignitaries prompted a Secret Service agent to request that he "get back on the other side of the rope."

I stepped over to the agent and said, "Let me introduce you to the mayor."

President Johnson's Lewiston speech was rambling. He talked about inflation and the need for "self-discipline" to control it. He talked about the good life being led by many Americans—high wages, good homes, and good schools. He said that "except for our problems in Vietnam, we have much to be thankful for." He mentioned the night that John Kennedy had come to the Lewiston park far behind schedule and said he understood that "you people waited almost four hours in almost zero weather."

I thought back. It had been longer than four hours. Ed Muskie had led songs and told stories in a virtuoso performance while awaiting JFK. It had been the Sunday night before the Tuesday elections in 1960 in which John F. Kennedy was to be elected president of the United States. The people of Lewiston stayed on through the cold hours, and finally Kennedy had come.

This summer evening in 1966, Lyndon Johnson went on a thirty-minute handshaking spree after he finished speaking, starting with the Job Corps girls down front who had presented a bouquet to Mrs. Johnson. As he was completing his rounds, I got into a State Police car already holding four troopers. They were to make a precautionary "sweep" of the Maine Turnpike to Portland in advance of the motorcade. I went along in order to check the Maine State Pier departure site with the crowd in place before the motorcade arrived there.

In Portland, 4,000 or 5,000 persons were jammed into the small open area and down the narrow piers to the gangplank. There was a band to ompah and a fenced VIP section for the local dignitaries. I lined them up and asked Nobles to make the introductions to the president. The motorcade arrived just as night was settling on the waterfront. When the introductions were made, LBJ took bullhorn in hand.

"We like your beautiful Maine," he said. "We like the people. We come here whenever we can."

As the party boarded the cruiser, Peter Kyros came up to me and asked, "Can you get me on that ship?" He had asked the same question several times before. I had explained that Muskie had set the terms with Watson, that nonpartisanship of a sort was being observed, and that his opponent would not be aboard, so Muskie had not insisted that he get a berth.

"I can't do a thing," I said, suggesting, however, that he move off the dock so that reporters or photographers would not notice him looking wistfully at the *Northampton*. He remained. Later I saw a copy of the *Portland Sunday Telegram* for August 21. There was a photograph of "a downcast Peter Kyros" standing on the dock. Maybe it helped him. He was elected.

My earned anonymity average, a matter of professional vanity to an experienced advance man, did not suffer on the trip. Despite my wide acquaintanceship in Maine, especially among newsmen and politicians, I did not get my name in the newspapers once. And I had kept reasonably clear of the news photographers. One shot in a Lewiston newspaper caught me introducing Mayor Couturier to President Johnson.

We went back to Brunswick Naval Air Station to board a backup aircraft that would be returning to Washington. Marty Underwood had flown in on that plane from other New England stops. We sat together talking about the 1964 campaign and our later activities. Marty had been traveling constantly. He was to stay with Lyndon Johnson to the end, turning out a crowd as private citizen Johnson left Andrews Air Force Base for Texas on the day of Richard Nixon's inauguration. I told Marty on the return to Washington from Brunswick that I had done enough advancing, that the Maine trip probably was my last one. The next two times I was sounded out, I had reasons to decline. The requests stopped coming.

There was a postscript to that last trip. Jim Jones called from the White House on the following September 27 asking about the arrangements that had been made to supply electricity to the bandstand area in Kennedy Park at Lewiston. I checked my notes and told him that the details for electrical service had been worked out by Major Frank Deguay of the White House Communications Agency and the Lewiston Public Works Department after I had talked with the mayor. Jones was asking because there was a story out of Maine on the UPI ticker. It went like this:

UPI-63
(LBJ BILL)
LEWISTON, MAINE—THE CITY OF LEWISTON IS PRESENTING PRESIDENT JOHNSON WITH A $748.77 BILL FOR POWER USED DURING A NONPOLITICAL TRIP HERE.
THE LEWISTON FINANCE BOARD AGREED LAST NIGHT TO SEEK PAYMENT FROM THE PRESIDENT. THE BOARD SAID THE MONEY WAS SPENT ON EXTRA LARGE AMOUNTS OF POWER TO PROVIDE LIGHTING FACILITIES AND POWER FOR RADIO AND TELEVISION COVERAGE DURING THE PRESIDENT'S VISIT.
IF THE TRIP HAD BEEN POLITICAL, SAID DEMOCRATIC MAYOR ROBERT L. COUTURIER, THE DEMOCRATS WOULD HAVE FOOTED THE BILL.
9/27—GE1143A

I got on the phone to George Mitchell: "George, President Johnson has been reading the news tickers, and guess what?" I read the piece to him. He took care of it.

Epilogue

As the world knows, the beginnings of the Democratic pre-campaign for the presidency in the 1964 election ended on November 22, 1963, in tragedy—the assassination of President John Fitzgerald Kennedy in Dallas, Texas. Advance men who were "trying out" on JFK's five-city trip in Texas for possible use when the real campaign got under way were left with a deep sadness for the young leader cut off in his prime. Lyndon Baines Johnson became their hope for a continued Democratic presidency.

The preceding pages have described the ways in which JFK was "advanced" in Fort Worth, his last stop before Dallas, and how LBJ was "advanced" on trips before, during, and after the campaign he won—with the emphasis on "during." What follows are some concluding reflections from the advance man's point of view.

John Fitzgerald Kennedy was mourned widely as a president of vigor, charm, and promise. His memory, unfortunately, has been diminished by continuing wild concoctions of conspiracy supposedly involved in his death, this despite the fact that over the years no sustainable evidence has been found that assassin Lee Harvey Oswald acted for anyone but himself. Gossip in the guise of research continues to blur the recollections of this spirited president who, in his shortened presidency, was responsible for such things as the founding of the Peace Corps, the facing down of Soviet Premier Khrushchev in the Cuban Missile Crisis, and the initiation of some of the key progressive legislation later enacted under President Johnson.

In a changed cultural climate, LBJ was able to sign into law the Civil Rights Act of 1964, followed by a cascade of additional progressive legislation, including the Voting Rights Act of 1965 and a variety of measures to reduce the impacts of poverty. His landslide victory in the 1964 election enabled him to address legislatively numerous subjects for social improvement. The scope of subjects was breathtaking: Head Start, Education, Medicare, Medicaid. The list goes on and on.

Passage owed much to the drive and legislative skills of Lyndon Johnson. Action was supported by the emotions that had swept the country in the wake of John Kennedy's assassination. Opposition to progressive legislation had weakened. The country was prepared to do good after an encounter with evil. Unfortunately, the domestic progress was seen against the backdrop of the Vietnam War, from which neither Presidents Kennedy nor Johnson extricated the United States. What did the advance unit of the Johnson campaign of 1964 have to do with the beneficent legislation of this period? There is a temptation to claim too much. Realistically, the most that can be said is that it helped elect Lyndon Johnson by a wide enough margin to show that the country was ready for change. A measure of Democratic Party unity was demonstrated by the strength of support for the party's legislative program in Congress, although strains between Kennedy and Johnson loyalists were evident elsewhere. The imperious dismantling of the Kennedy-dominated Democratic National Committee during the Johnson presidency was a particular sore point for many New Frontiersmen. However, much common ground was shared by the two administrations.

As 1964 progressed, Johnson's fellow Texan, W. Marvin Watson, served more and more as LBJ's White House overseer—he would become the president's chief of staff after the election. Watson had emerged as the dominant voice in the White House after the president's. He was completely loyal to the president and adamant in enforcing LBJ's wishes, such as Johnson's apparent demand that advance men do something about Goldwater signs at LBJ rallies.

The first lesson in presidential advancing learned at Fort Worth was that an apprentice could make mistakes, but keeping as many people as possible happy, or at least not angry, would cover a multitude of sins of omission. There was much more to learn. The advance man started out in a new territory like Willie Loman with a smile on his face and a shine on his shoes, but eventually there were many hands. The trappings of an American president in the 1960s were impressive, from transportation on. However, the advance men who took assignments for motorcades for granted, or believed promises at their telling, did so at their peril. An advance man, by definition, checks things out.

Rewards. There were, though, certain satisfactions to experience: a sharp feeling of elation, almost euphoric, coupled with relief following a difficult stop at which the crowds proved thick and cheering, the arrangements polished, and no disgruntled factions left behind.

And yet. *And yet.* Although the advance man might find that preparing the way—mostly physically—for a president seeking to hold on to what he had was not an intellectual exercise of a very high order, he could at least justify himself as a servant of the democratic process and feel virtuous as well as clever. Or could he? I sometimes thought back to doubts.

What was it that was unsettling about taking part in the old American custom of turning out crowds to greet a politician, of assembling men and women and children en masse to clap and cheer, encouraging them to shout slogans such as "All the way with LBJ" as others had chanted "Bryan, Bryan, Bryan" and "We Want Willkie," handing them "spontaneous" signs that had been scrawled with care in a backroom of the party's state committee headquarters? It was the uneasy feeling that a contribution was being made to the mindlessness of America, that once again the "blunt monster with uncounted heads" was being summoned up, the mob marshaled along the pavements to scratch an ultracrepidarian itch. It was the awareness that the emotional exploitation of men massed can become almost overpowering in political campaigns when the urge to win tyrannously commands. So you come to terms with reality but wish that there were less blather and more substance in presidential campaigns.

Ecclesiastes tells us there is a time for this and a time for that. The time for political advancing for some of us came when there were two presidents with sound domestic visions to serve and the opportunity to lend a hand in a minor way. A regret remains that the Democratic presidents of the 1960s were unable to stop U.S. involvement in an unnecessary war of their time.

Appendix

Political campaign advancing, particularly of the presidential type recounted here, has come a long way since the 1960s. Beginning with the Nixon administration, the White House has had a separate Advance Office to coordinate presidential trips, political and nonpolitical. This was a change from the less structured travel systems of the JFK and LBJ presidential years.

In the 1964 campaign there was very heavy reliance on volunteers as advance men to bolster the small number recruited from the government for the LBJ advance unit. There were about forty-five volunteers, but only a dozen were selected for the key campaign appearances after they had proved their worth at minor "stops." Few of the advance men were deeply experienced in that aspect of campaigning before signing on to the LBJ unit. Advancing was an episode in their lives, not a career.

There was a strong flavor of the Peace Corps in the LBJ advance unit. This was understandable in that the man in overall charge was Bill D. Moyers, deputy director of the Peace Corps before becoming a principal aide to President Johnson. Moreover, the "hands-on" manager of the advance was Wilson McCarthy, who had been doing congressional relations for the Peace Corps.

Where did the key advance men go after the campaign "episode?" Moyers was a newspaper publisher for a time and eventually became a well-known television pundit. McCarthy went to Hollywood and did public relations for MGM, while living in style in Malibu. When in New York he was based at the Waldorf Astoria. Later he and his family moved to England, where he wrote novels. Times became harder for the McCarthy family, and friends say there was a bout with alcoholism. He wrote two novels and was working on a third in Canada, where the McCarthys had moved by then. He died there on June 12, 1981. His first novel, *The Detail*, had been named after the Secret Service's White House Detail, with which he had been closely associated in campaign days. Warner Brothers considered the novel as a possible movie, but that did not happen. Wilson McCarthy—he should be remembered for the good job he did for LBJ in the '64 election.

Two other principal advance men who were Peace Corps alumni, Harold (Hal) Pachios and Padraic (Pat) Kennedy, were among those with substantial post-election careers. Pachios was an assistant to Bill Moyers when the latter was LBJ's press secretary. Then, after a period on the legal staff of the federal Department of Transportation, Pachios returned to Maine to practice law, and he became a founding partner of a law firm with offices in Portland and Augusta. After the '64 election, LBJ appointed Pat Kennedy as director of Vista, the domestic Peace Corps. Later, for twenty-seven years, Kennedy was CEO of the planned community of Columbia in Maryland.

Jerry Bruno, who played a strong role in the '64 LBJ advance unit, is principally remembered as the high-profile advance man for the presidential campaigns of John Kennedy in 1960 and Robert Kennedy in 1968. He became a popular lecturer on political campaigns at colleges and universities. Mel Cottone, who had begun working on national campaigns in West Virginia during JFK's run for the presidency, became a fixture in Washington campaigns.

The enigma in the Democratic advance annals of the 1960s was Martin E. (Marty) Underwood, who shared with me the position of deputy director of the LBJ advance unit in '64. Underwood, who had been the advance man for JFK in Houston on November 21, 1963, stayed with LBJ as an advance man through LBJ's term as president. He was an amiable friend and accomplished advance man—but with problems. At times in the '64 campaign he was a binge drinker and was known to associates over the years for embellishing his roles to credulous interviewers.

Underwood's contradictory accounts, if taken seriously, would further muddle the history of the JFK assassination era. His tale of eliciting from the CIA station chief in Mexico City the details of Cuban instigation and involvement in JFK's assassination was one of his later stories. It was sometimes told as true, sometimes denied—the latter when an official record was involved. This tale has spawned books and a film documentary about the assassination. I much prefer to remember him as a friend and as a competent advance man rather than as a reliable historic source—which he was not. McCarthy asked me at one point if I knew that Underwood had a hobby of collecting information about con men. I did not, but I was not surprised by McCarthy's information. Underwood died on March 18, 2003.

The other deputy of the advance unit, this writer, went back to civil service after the '64 election. My last job before retirement from the government was, for eight years, director of the Federal Register, publishing the nation's laws, regulations, and presidential documents— oh, and overseeing the documentation of the Electoral College voting. All ex post facto information. No advance work involved.

Name Index

04-09-2010 — DEh